COMPLETE GUIDE
VERSAILLES

© Édition Art Lys

Coordination: Denis Kilian
Layout: Aline Hudelot
Production: Pierre Kegels, Christian Ryo
Documentation : Christian Ryo
Scheduling: Thierry Lebreton, Dominique Bissière

Photographs:
RMN/Lewandowski
RMN/G. Blot
Artephot/Varga
Art Lys/É. Burnier
Art Lys/J. Girard

ISBN 2-854 95-051-8
Achevé d'imprimer le 15 septembre 1998
par la STIGE (CEE)
Dépôt légal septembre 1998

COMPLETE GUIDE
VERSAILLES

SIMONE HOOG,
Head Curator in charge of Heritage

DANIEL MEYER,
Head Curator

of the Versailles and Trianon
National Museums

CONTENTS

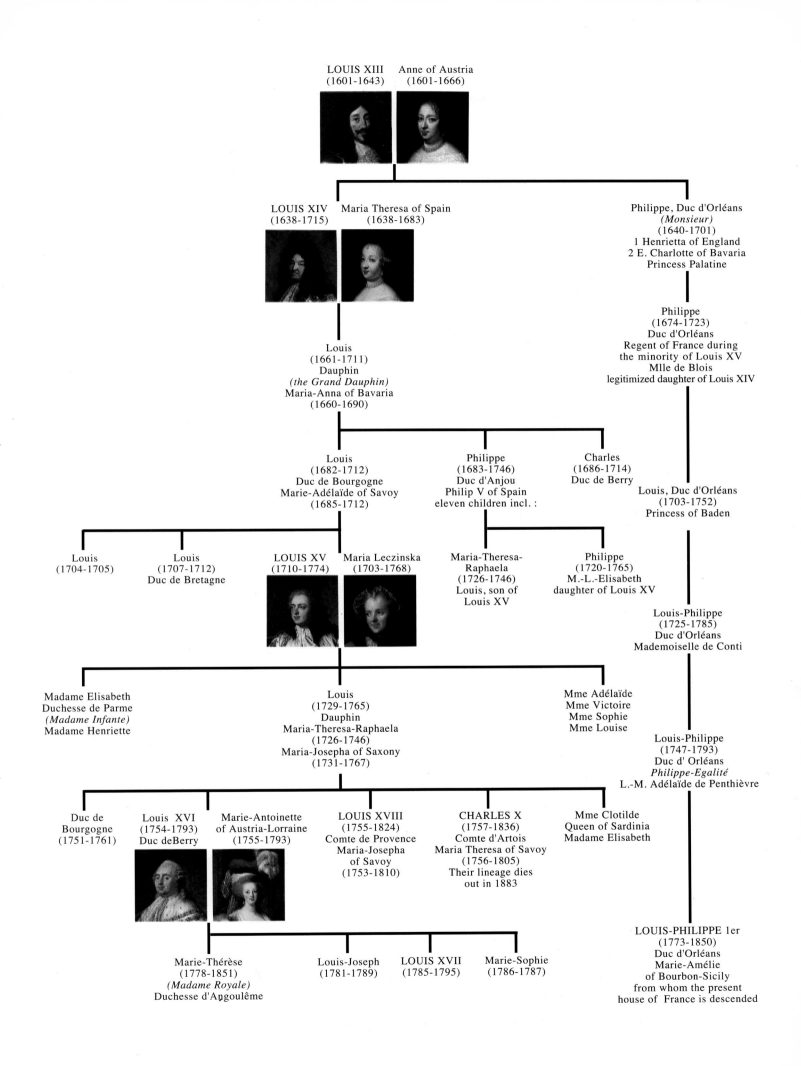

LOUIS XIII
(1601-1643)

Anne of Austria
(1601-1666)

LOUIS XIV
(1638-1715)

Maria Theresa of Spain
(1638-1683)

Philippe, Duc d'Orléans
(Monsieur)
(1640-1701)
1 Henrietta of England
2 E. Charlotte of Bavaria
Princess Palatine

Louis
(1661-1711)
Dauphin
(the Grand Dauphin)
Maria-Anna of Bavaria
(1660-1690)

Philippe
(1674-1723)
Duc d'Orléans
Regent of France during
the minority of Louis XV
Mlle de Blois
legitimized daughter of Louis XIV

Louis
(1682-1712)
Duc de Bourgogne
Marie-Adélaïde of Savoy
(1685-1712)

Philippe
(1683-1746)
Duc d'Anjou
Philip V of Spain
eleven children incl. :

Charles
(1686-1714)
Duc de Berry

Louis, Duc d'Orléans
(1703-1752)
Princess of Baden

Louis
(1704-1705)

Louis
(1707-1712)
Duc de Bretagne

LOUIS XV
(1710-1774)

Maria Leczinska
(1703-1768)

Maria-Theresa-
Raphaela
(1726-1746)
Louis, son of
Louis XV

Philippe
(1720-1765)
M.-L.-Elisabeth
daughter of Louis XV

Louis-Philippe
(1725-1785)
Duc d'Orléans
Mademoiselle de Conti

Madame Elisabeth
Duchesse de Parme
(Madame Infante)
Madame Henriette

Louis
(1729-1765)
Dauphin
Maria-Theresa-Raphaela
(1726-1746)
Maria-Josepha of Saxony
(1731-1767)

Mme Adélaïde
Mme Victoire
Mme Sophie
Mme Louise

Louis-Philippe
(1747-1793)
Duc d' Orléans
Philippe-Egalité
L.-M. Adélaïde de Penthièvre

Duc de
Bourgogne
(1751-1761)

Louis XVI
(1754-1793)
Duc deBerry

Marie-Antoinette
of Austria-Lorraine
(1755-1793)

LOUIS XVIII
(1755-1824)
Comte de Provence
Maria-Josepha
of Savoy
(1753-1810)

CHARLES X
(1757-1836)
Comte d'Artois
Maria Theresa of Savoy
(1756-1805)
Their lineage dies
out in 1883

Mme Clotilde
Queen of Sardinia
Madame Elisabeth

Marie-Thérèse
(1778-1851)
(Madame Royale)
Duchesse d'Angoulême

Louis-Joseph
(1781-1789)

LOUIS XVII
(1785-1795)

Marie-Sophie
(1786-1787)

LOUIS-PHILIPPE 1er
(1773-1850)
Duc d'Orléans
Marie-Amélie
of Bourbon-Sicily
from whom the present
house of France is descended

VERSAILLES,

HOME OF THE OLD MONARCHY

Long before becoming a symbol of France's power in Europe, and the setting for spectacular festivities held by Louis XVI, Versailles was but a simple hunting pavilion.

As of 1661, when the personal reign of Louis XIV began, this small country residence favored by Louis XIII became a veritable château surrounded by gardens. The village of Versailles followed the palace's development to became a real city. And, in 1682, this estate, located far from Paris, was chosen by the monarch as the permanent residence of the Court and the Government.

Versailles, as we see and visit it today, gives an idea of the extent of France's influence during the 17th and 18th centuries.

Relatively little is known of the original hunting pavilion which Louis XIII had erected in 1623. Bassompierre, a French diplomat, described it as a: «miserable constrtuction of which a simple gentlemen would not boast.»

Yet, it was so pleasantly situated that, in 1631, Louis XIll asked Philibert Le Roy to build a larger château, entirely of brick and stone, with raised slate roofing. This «house of cards», as Saint-Simon referred to it in his Memoirs, still flanks the Marble courtyard.

LOUIS XIV'S GRANDIOSE PROJECT

Louis XIV, enchanted by the little château of Versailles, decided as early as 1661 to have it renovated so that he could live there more comfortably. He enlisted the help of the landscape gardener Le Nôtre, the architect Le Vau and the painter Le Brun who spent the greater part of their careers enlarging and embellishing Versailles.

To this wondrous estate, Louis XIV wished to add the prestige offered by music and literature. Over a ten-year period, the King held three unforgettable festivities highlighted by presentations of works by the best artists of the time, names such as Molière and Lully.

The first of these, Pleasures of the Enchanted Island, took place in May 1664. The theme of the celebrations was taken from two epic poems of the 16th century: Orlando furioso by Ariosto and Gerusalemme liberata by Tasso. Molière produced The Princess of Elis and the first three acts of Tartuffe.

The second celebration, and the most famous of the trilogy, was held on July 18, l668; it is known as the Great Royal Entertainment of Versailles and was marked by the creation of two works: Georges Dandin by Molière and Les Fêtes de l'Amour et de Bacchus by Lully.

The last great celebration was held in July 1674. It included several operas by Lully, and also Le Malade imaginaire, by Molière and, on August 18, Racine's Iphigénia was performed in the orangery.

In 1668, after the Great Royal Entertainment, Louis XIV decided to enlarge Versailles «in order to live there comfortably with his Council for several days.»

The ensuing project was led by the architect Le Vau who erected, on the garden side, a stone «envelope» around three sides of Louis XIII's château.

1661
Cardinal Mazarin dies and
the personal reign of Louis XIV begins.

1663
The architect Le Vau builds the first
orangery and begins the Menagerie.

1665
First statues placed in the gardens.
Thetis grotto completed .

1667
Excavation of the Grand Canal begins.
Le Nôtre makes first enlargement
of the central avenue.

1668
Le Vau's project to enlarge
the château on the garden side by
building a «stone envelope» is retained.

1670
The Porcelain Trianon is built.

1624
Louis XlII has a hunting pavilion
built on the slopes of Versailles.

1631
Louis XIII asks Philibert Le Roy to
build a small château on the site
of the hunting pavilion.

1672
Work begins on the Bathing
Apartments and the
Ambassadors'Staircase.

1674
Colbert commissions 24 statues
designed by Le Brun for the gardens.

1678

J. Hardouin-Mansart presents his project to expand the château: it includes replacing the terrace onto the gardens by the Hall of Mirrors, and buiding the North and South wings.

1681

Le Brun completes decoration of the State Apartments. Construction of the Marly water works.

1682

Louis XIV decrees Versailles the seat of Government and the official residence of the Court.

1684

Hall of Mirrors completed. Construction of the orangery. Thetis grotto demolished.

1685

Construction of the North Wing begins.

1687

Construction of the Marble Trianon by Hardouin-Mansart

1710

Consecration of the Royal Chapel.

1715

September 1, Louis XIV dies. September 9, Louis XV forsakes Versailles for Vincennes.

1722

Louis XV takes up residence in Versailles.

1738

Large-scale work begun on the Private Apartments.

In the newly built North Wing, the King's State Apartments were created, and, in the South Wing side, those of the Queen, with a large terrace between them, overlooking the gardens.

The new Royal Courtyard, which extended the existing Marble Courtyard, was closed off by a semicircular railing, and new buildings linking the wings to the kitchens and the stables were built. Four pavilions stood in each corner of the large entrance courtyard; they were linked by Mansart to create the Ministers' Wings.

Shortly after Le Vau's death in 1670, the architect Jules Hardouin-Mansart took over direction of the construction work. His desire for architectural grandeur. corresponded exactly to the Sun King's tastes, and after Le Brun's death in 1690, he became the all-powerful master of the King's buildings at Versailles.

Between 1682 and 1686, he extended the South and North Wings on the garden side to create a facade roughly 2200 feet long.

In 1678, the terrace as well as the King's and Queen's cabinets on the first floor of the central building were replaced by the large ensemble formed by the Hall of Mirrors, the War Drawing-Room and the Peace Drawing-Room .

On the Marble Courtyard side, another storey was added to the central building in 1679. The facade was crowned by a clock framed by the statues of Mars by Marsy and Hercules by Girardon. The other statues along the balustrade were also added at that time.

Inside the château, Mansart built the Queen's Staircase in the South Wing to match the Ambassadors' Staircase begun by Le Vau in the North Wing (but demolished in 1752).

The King's Apartments overlooking the Marble Courtyard were altered in 1701, and their layout was the same as it is today: the King's Bedchamber in the center of the château between the Bull's Eye Drawing-Room and the Council Cabinet, which has since been enlarged.

The Royal Chapel, consecrated in 1710, was the last major body of work executed during Louis XIV's lifetime.

THE SUCCESSORS OF LOUIS XIV

Upon Louis XIV's death in 1715, the Versailles of our day had already taken shape in its general outward appearance. The successors of the Sun King altered only the interior decor of the apartments.

In 1722, Louis XV, the great-grandson of l.ouis XIV, declared Versailles his royal residence. Inaugurated in 1736, the Hercules Drawing-Room boasts a splendid ceiling, painted by Lemoine. The King's Private Apartments on the first floor of the North Wing, overlooking the Marble Courtyard, were decorated in a more intimate style.

Although the changes made by Louis XV involved the disappearance of some of the rooms which were such a source of wonder to visitors of Louis XIV's time, they resulted, nevertheless, in the creation of the King's charming Cabinets. Here, the artists surpassed themselves in their zeal and elegance as they worked under the direction of the architect and decorator Jacques-Ange Gabriel. It was the same architect who, after designing several projects, built the fine opera of Versailles concealed in the North Wing of the château. It was inaugurated in 1770 for the marriage of the Dauphin to the Archduchess Marie-Antoinette.

Gabriel then planned on rebuilding the courtyard side of the château. All that remains of his project is the wing named after him, with its classical fronton supported by a colonnade to the right of the entrance courtyard.

Unlike his ancestors, Louis XVI took no great intersest in building. The only changes made during his reign were to the palace's interior decor, particularly the Queen's private suite which ran along his State Apartment.

VERSAILLES, A MODEL FOR THE REST OF EUROPE

Everyday life at Versailles followed the pace set by the King's life, itself regulated to the minutest detail by the laws of Etiquette. The King's every action and gesture were the pretext for a ceremony: his rising and retiring, his meal or his walk in the gardens. A dazzling audience was present when the King heard Mass or granted an audience to an ambassador. The Court filled the palace with life and constant motion. To entertain their courtiers, the Kings held magnificent festivities. They included theatrical performances, operas, and masked or fulldress balls held in the apartments, the Hall of Mirrors or the park. In Marie-Antoinette's time, the Trianon was the setting for many illuminations (light shows).

The greatness of Versailles radiated all over Europe at the end of 17th and throughout the 18th century. Versailles became a source of inspiration for architects designing new palaces for their sovereigns; some of their creations were Sans-Souci, Potsdam, Schönbrunn, Caserta. During the last century, Louis II of Bavaria had the central building of the château and the parterres reproduced for his own purposes.

VERSAILLES A MUSEUM DEDICATED TO «ALL THE GLORIES OF FRANCE»

After the revolution of July 1830, which brought Louis-Philippe d'Orléans to power, the Chamber of Deputies voted a law placing the estate of Versailles and the Trianon on the Civil List. Almost immediately Louis-Philippe ordered the creation at Versailles of a Museum dedicated to «All the Glories of France.» It was inaugurated on june 1, 1837. Today, Versailles continues to play its part as a historical museum. In the North Wing, the 17th century rooms are a prelude to the tour of the State Apartments; this visit may be continued by visiting the Hall of Battles and the rooms in the South Wing dedicated to the Napoleonic epic. The renovated 18th and 19th century rooms complete this vast panorama of our history.

VERSAILLES TODAY

After the departure of the monarchy, the art inspired by Versailles almost came to a complete stop. However, by means of important technical advances, an attempt is being made in our time to revive the entire royal estate.

Of course, many changes made during the 19th century altered the château interior but today the Curatorial and Architecture Departments of Versailles are attempting to restore life to it by gradually refurnishing the rooms which the Revolution had emptied, by patiently restoring and consolidating the structure of this monument which time and past indifference, albeit brief, did not spare.

1768
The architect].-A. Gabriel completes the Small Trianon.

1770
Inauguration of the Opera built by Gabriel.

1771
New project focuses on rebuilding all of the château's facades facing the city. Gabriel begins the Louis XV Wing.

1774
Louis XV dies of smallpox at Versailles. Louis XVI gives orders to replant the park.

1783
Marie-Antoinette's Hamlet built by Richard Mique.

1789
May 5, opening of the States General in the Menus Plaisirs room. October 6, the King, the Royal Family and the entire Court leave Versailles definitively for Paris

1814
Louis XVIII has the château's apartments renovated.

1837
June 18, inauguration of the Versailles Museum by Louis-Philippe.

1871
January 18, the King of Prussia is proclaimed Emperor of Germany in the Hall of Mirrors. In March, during the uprising of the Commune, the House of Commons holds its sessions in the opera.

1919
June 28, The Versailles Treaty ending World War I is signed in the Hall of Mirrors

THE MUSEUM

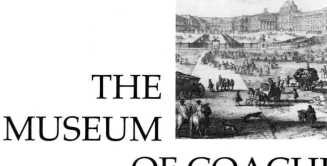

OF COACHES

Accommodated in the Great Stable, the Museum of Coaches exhibits a collection of cars chiefly assembled by Louis-Philippe when he turned the château of Versailles into a museum dedicated to all of the glories of France. Of the cars recorded on the old civil list, he purchased those of historic interest. Thus, the berlins of the wedding of Napoleon I arrived at the museum, seven gala carriages reminiscent of the magnificence of the Imperial Court at its pinnacle, on April 2, 1810. Or the coach of the anointing of Charles X, designed by Piercier, Architect for Louis XVIII who did not dare use the carriage in the politically hostile context of the Restauration. Louis-Philippe also acquired sleighs and sedans. In 1833, the hearse of Louis XVIII was added to the collection then kept at the Small Stable. Used for the funeral of Marshal Lannes, Duke of Montebello, in 1809, it underwent transformations, and carried the mortal remains of the Duke of Berry (son of king-to-be Charles X), assassinated in 1820. The carriage was then refurbished for the funeral of Louis XVIII on September 23, 1824. Though it was used again on several occasions thereafter, it is to its condition on that date that it has been restored.

CHATEAUBRIAND, MÉMOIRES D'OUTRE-TOMBE (MEMOIRS FROM BEYOND THE GRAVE) I saw the King enter, I saw gilded carriages go by, of a monarch who once had no mount. I saw carriages drive by full of courtiers who never had to stand up for their master. The dregs went to sing the *Te Deum*, and I went to see Roman ruins...

HEARSE OF LOUIS XVIII

DESIGNED BY LECOINTE AND HITTOFF

COACH OF THE ANOINTING OF CHARLES X

DESIGNED BY PERCIER

10

First-floor Plan of the Chateau

The State Apartment
1 Drawing Room of Plenty
2 Venus Drawing Room
3 Diana Drawing Room
4 Mars Drawing Room
5 Mercury Drawing Room
6 Apollo Drawing Room
7 War Drawing Room

The Queen's Apartment
8 Peace Drawing Room
9 Queen's Bedchamber
10 State Cabinet or Salon des Nobles
11 Antechamber of the Grand Couvert
12 Guard Room
13 Marble or Queen's Staircase
14 Loggia (also leading to the King's Apartment)

The Queen's Private Rooms
a Bathroom
b Annexe to Library
c Private Cabinet
d Library
e Meridian Cabinet
f The Duchesse de Bourgogne's Cabinet

Madame de Maintenon's Apartment
g-h Antechambers
i Bedchamber
j State Cabinet

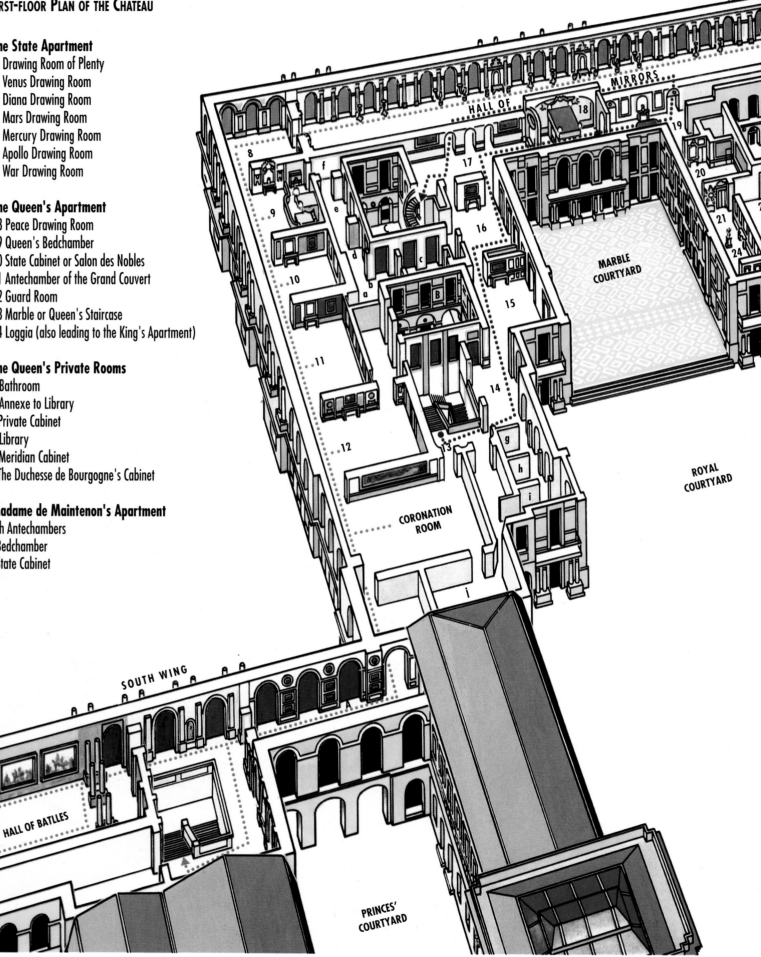

HALL OF MIRRORS

MARBLE COURTYARD

ROYAL COURTYARD

CORONATION ROOM

SOUTH WING

HALL OF BATTLES

PRINCES' COURTYARD

The King's Apartment
15 Guard Room
16 First Antechamber or Grand Couvert
17 Second Antechamber or Œuil-de-Bœuf
18 King's Bedchamber
19 Council Chamber

The King's Private Apartment
20 Bedroom
21 Clock Cabinet
22 Antichambre des Chiens
23 Private Dining Room
24 Private Cabinet
25 Arrière-cabinet
26 Cabinet de la Vaiselle d'Or
27 Bathroom
28 Louis XVI's Library
29 Dining Room (New Rooms)
30 Buffet Room
31 Louis XVI's Games Room

A 1792 Room
B Monseigneur's or Queen's Courtyard
C Dauphin's or Queen's Courtyard
D Cour des Cerfs (Courtyard of the Stags)
E The King's Staircase
F The King's Private Courtyard
G Royal Gallery of the Chapel
H 17th-Century Rooms

.... Tour of the State Apartments
.... Tour of King's Bedchamber

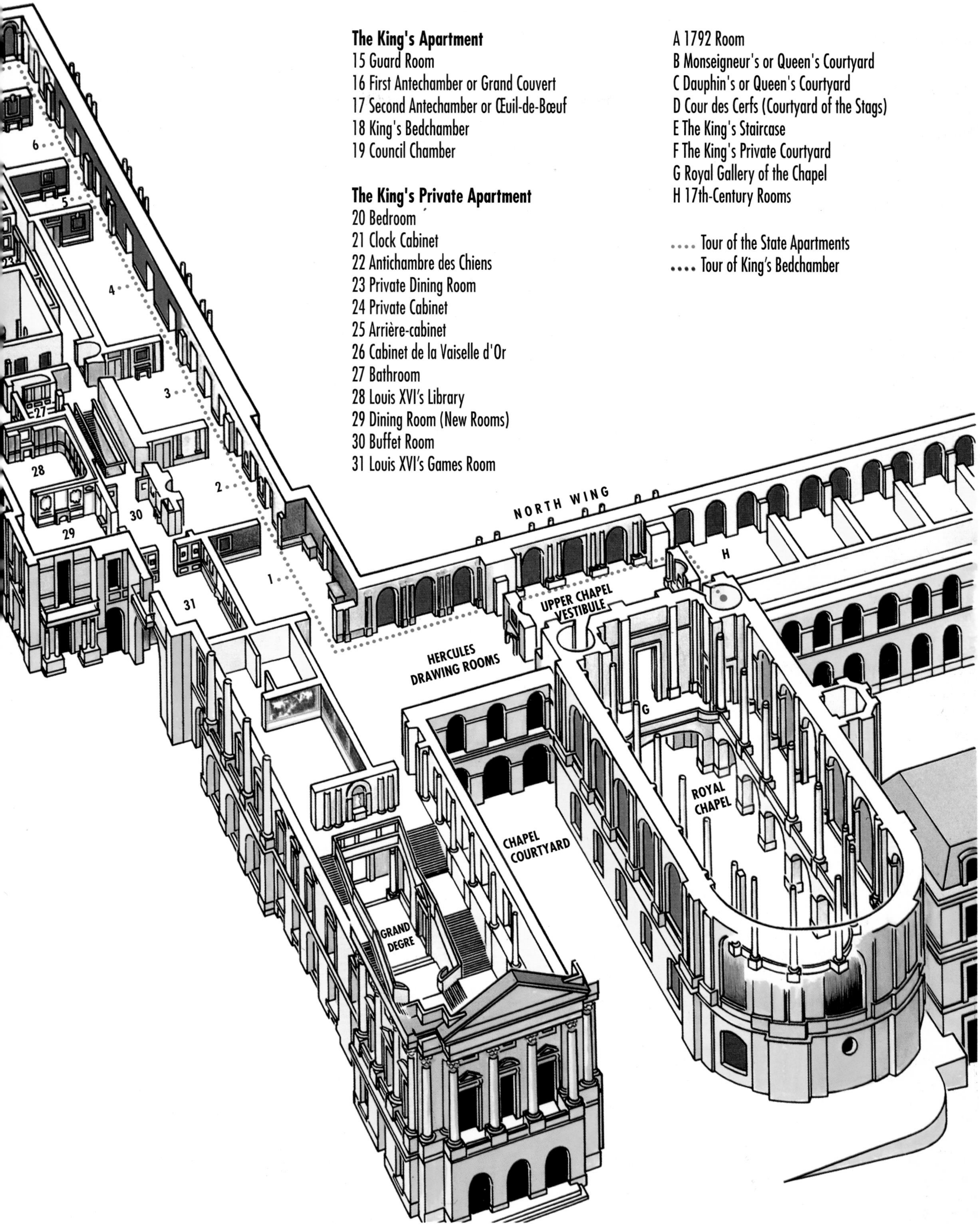

NORTH WING

UPPER CHAPEL
VESTIBULE

HERCULES
DRAWING ROOMS

CHAPEL
COURTYARD

G

ROYAL
CHAPEL

GRAND
DEGRE

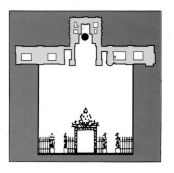

THE COURTYARDS

Three wide, tree-lined avenues converge onto the château, the Avenue de Saint-Cloud (to the north), the Avenue de Paris (in the middle) and the Avenue de Sceaux (to the south). These avenues are flanked by the Great Stables (to the north) and the Small Stables (to the south) built by Hardouin-Mansart starting in 1679.

Crossing the Place d'Armes, the visitor passes through the main gateway, adorned with the Royal Arms of France, and into the Ministers' Courtyard flanked by the two Ministers' Wings, built in 1671 and 1679. On either side of the gateway stand four sets of sculptures dedicated to War, with the King's Victories over the Empire and Spain, and Peace, with Peace and Plenty. Under the Ancient Regime (pre-1789), these two sculptures were on either side of the railings that separated the Ministers' Courtyard from the Royal Courtyard. This second gateway, destroyed during the Revolution, was located where the equestrian statue of Louis XIV (installed in 1837 under Louis-Philippe's reign) now stands. It was connected to two pavilions, replaced to the north by the Louis XV Wing designed by Gabriel, and to the south by the Dufour Pavilion (erected under Louis XVIII). Only a small number of lords, those who had the right to the "Honors of the Louvre", were permitted to enter the Royal Courtyard by coach. Closer to the palace and up five steps, the Marble Courtyard, paved with slabs of black and white marble, is the same size as the courtyard of Louis XIII's original château.

THE COUNT OF HÉZECQUES, RECOLLECTIONS OF A PAGE IN LOUIS XVI'S COURT.
"The door guards were supposed to guard the main gateway to the royal courtyard, but only during the day. They only opened it at the hour given for the rising of the King, usually at eleven thirty. They were also supposed to know who had the right to drive their coaches up into this courtyard. This favour, called the honors of the Louvre, was reserved for princes, field-marshals and ambassadors."

THE MARBLE COURTYARD

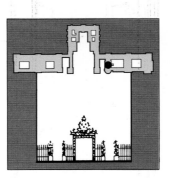

THE ROYAL CHAPEL

The Royal Chapel is the château's fifth chapel, but the first to occupy a separate building, as the earlier ones had always formed part of the château itself. Situated near the angle formed by the château's central section and the North Wing, it was constructed by Jules Hardouin-Mansart from 1699 until his death in 1708, and completed in 1710 by his brother-in-law, Robert de Cotte.

It has two storeys, like the traditional Palatine chapels, but its style is classical in inspiration. The decoration draws a parallel between the Old and New Testament. This is seen in the reliefs by the Coustou brothers, Frémin, Lemoine, Van Clève, Magnier, Poirier and Vassé, and in the vaulted ceiling's paintings devoted to the Holy Trinity: *The Resurrection of Christ*, in the apse, by La Fosse, *Glory to God the Father*, in the center of the nave, by Antoine Coypel, *The Descent of the Holy Spirit*, above the royal gallery, by Jouvenet, and in the organ loft's decor representing King David.

The King of France would hear Mass from the gallery opposite the altar. This gallery was on the same floor as his apartments, and he entered the lower half of the chapel only for important occasions.

To reach the gallery, the King would go through a room decorated in stone with a vaulted ceiling supported by columns and pilasters with Corinthian capitals. This vestibule was built at the same time as the Chapel with a similar stone decor; it connects the Chapel to the State Apartment. One of the two niches contains a statue of Glory holding a medallion of Louis XV by Vassé, the other the statue of Magnanimity, by Bousseau.

The Royal Chapel, dedicated to Saint Louis, was the setting for ceremonies of the Order of the Holy Spirit, the Te Deum was sung here for military victories and births of the children of France, and the Princes of the Blood were married here.

PRINCESSE PALATINE, VERSAILLES, FEBRUARY 20, 1695. "It is a great honor to be seated next to the King during the sermon, but I would gladly surrender my place as H.M. will not let nap; as soon as I fall asleep, the King nudges my elbow and wakes me up."

THE ALTAR AND ORGAN LOFT

SAINT-SIMON, MEMOIRS. "The King attended Mass, where his musicians always sang a motet. He went downstairs only for major festivities, or for ceremonies. On the way to or from Mass, anyone could talk to him if he wished, but less distinguished persons had to clear the Captain of the Guards first, and he went there and back by the door of the cabinets in the Hall. During Mass, the ministers were notified, and they assembled in the King's chamber, where dignitaries could meet them and talk. The King had little time for amusement after Mass, and almost always convened the Council straightaway. And that completed the morning."

KING DAVID
PLAYING
THE HARP

CHAPEL
OF THE HOLY
SACRAMENT

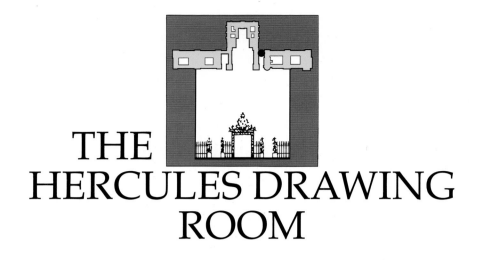

THE HERCULES DRAWING ROOM

This expansive drawing room linking the North Wing to the central building of the château was the setting for sparkling receptions. "It was installed in the top part of the fourth chapel (used from 1682 to 1710)". The decoration was entrusted to Robert de Cotte, who began the task in 1712. Work was interrupted in 1715 by the death of Louis XIV and only resumed in 1725.

The walls are covered with marble of different hues and punctuated with 20 pilasters with gilt bronze pedestals and Corinthian capitals. These support a cornice adorned with consoles and trophies.

Above the Antin marble fireplace hangs Veronese's Eliezer and Rebecca. Another painting by Veronese hangs opposite it: The Meal in the House of Simon the Pharisee; it was presented to Louis XIV by the Venetian Republic in 1664.

The ceiling, painted by François Lemoine from 1733 to 1736, portrays the apotheosis of Hercules; it earned the artist the title of Head Painter to the King.

DUC DE LUYNES, MEMOIRS.

"Just a few days ago, a learned man told me that when Lemoyne began working on the Hercules drawing room, he painted with as much precision and perfection as he would have for a canvas about to be closely examined.

When he had almost finished his work, he wanted to see the effect it had produced; he climbed down the scaffolding; from below he noticed that the wide cornice cut off his drawing and his characters; he was so struck by this that he erased everything. He then redid the same work, but used broad strokes; and although he did not add such perfection as he had to the previous attempt, he nevertheless thought he had done very well. Mr. d'Antin named him Head Painter to the King and gave him 10 000 ecus for the Hercules drawing room. However, his expenses alone amounted to 29 000 pounds; he had spent 24 000 pounds on ultramarine alone. This sum became an obsession and was the cause of his tragic end [he committed suicide]."

NORTH PART OF THE HERCULES DRAWING ROOM CEILING

DEZALLIER D'ARGENVILLE, SCENIC TRIP AROUND THE OUTSKIRTS OF PARIS.

"Lemoine's work is divided into nine groups composed of 142 characters. In the first group, Jupiter and Juno present Hercules, her future husband, to the young Hebe. In the second, Bacchus leans on the god Pan [_]. Mercury and Amphitrite are seen above; while Venus with the Graces and Eros, Pandora and Diana are lower down. [_] The third group consists of Mars, Vulcan and cupids. [_] Envy, Anger, Hatred, Discord, and other Vices, brought to the ground beside Hercules' chariot, make up the fourth. [_] The fifth group shows Cybele in a chariot, Minerva and Ceres, Neptune and Pluto. In the sixth, one can see Aeolus, Zephyr and Flora, Dew leaning over her urn on the clouds [_], above, Dreams spread poppies over the sleeping Morpheus. The seventh group represents Iris with Dawn surrounded by four Stars personified. Apollo with his Muses compose the eighth group. [_] In the ninth group, we see the constellations of Castor and Pollux. Silenus, followed by a band of children and fauns, holds a Bacchanalian revelry in honor of Hercules."

THE FIREPLACE IS DECORATED WITH LIONS SKINS AND A HEAD OF HERCULES

THE HERCULES DRAWING ROOM

THE STATE APARTMENT

DRAWING ROOM
OF PLENTY
VENUS DRAWING ROOM
DIANA DRAWING ROOM
MARS DRAWING ROOM
MERCURY
DRAWING ROOM
APOLLO DRAWING ROOM

The King's State Apartment, on the first floor of the château, overlooks the North Parterre. It was begun in 1671 and completed in 1681. Its purpose was not defined until 1682 when the King made Versailles his Court and seat of government.

This apartment, "where the King receives but does not live", was entered from the Ambassadors' Staircase, whose two flights led to the Venus and Diana Drawing rooms. Designed by Le Vau, the Ambassadors' Staircase was built by François d'Orbay and demolished in 1752, during the reign of Louis XV.

Before the Hall of Mirrors was built in 1678, the King's State Apartment unfolded in a lavish suite of seven rooms. Félibien, in 1674, described its sumptuous painted decor: "Since the Sun is the King's emblem, the seven planets were taken as the subjects of the paintings in the seven rooms which compose this apartment."

MODEL OF THE AMBASSADOR'S STAIRCASE

DRAWING ROOM OF PLENTY

When the Chapel occupied the site of the Hercules Drawing room, this room served as an entrance hall to the galleries. It also gave access to the Cabinet of Curios and Rare Objects. The collections it contained inspired the decor of the ceiling, painted by Le Brun; in the center is an allegory of Royal Magnificence, and all around the edge are silver and gold ware set out on a simulated balustrade. Some of these treasures are now on display in the Louvre.

ROYAL MAGNIFICENCE

DRAWING ROOM OF PLENTY

FÉLIBIEN, BRIEF DESCRIPTION OF VERSAILLES "If you look carefully at the King's nef above the mantelpiece, its two matching cruet-shaped vases, and the various pieces in gold and silver, amber and coral, placed one after the other, you will see that all of these works are covered in pearls, diamonds, rubies, emeralds, sapphires, turquoises, jacinth, garnets, opals and topaz. [...] But who can imagine the number and beauty of cameos and gems engraved in relief or intaglio? These precious monuments to Antiquity and the many medals, which give this room its name, constitute its greatest wealth."

THE VENUS DRAWING ROOM

This and the following room were reached by the Ambassadors' Staircase, demolished in 1752. It was here that, on evenings when the King held court in his apartment, a light supper was served on several tables set out along the walls.

The name of the Venus Drawing room comes from the ceiling painting, by R.-A. Houasse, depicting *Venus Subjugating the Gods and Powers*. The oval in the center portrays Venus in her chariot, crowned by the three Graces. She holds garlands of roses entwined around Mars, Vulcan, Bacchus, Neptune and Jupiter. These garlands extend into the corners of the ceiling, where they are used by cupids to unite Titus and Berenice, Antony and Cleopatra, Jason and Medea, Theseus and Ariadne.

On either side of the central motif, two monochrome paintings on a gold background depict *The Abduction of Europa by*

THE SUPREMACY OF VENUS

Jupiter metamorphosed into a Bull, and Amphitrite on a Dolphin's Back.
In the coves and throughout the State Apartment, classical themes evoke events of Louis XIV's reign: *Augustus presiding over the Circus Games* recalls the 1662 carousel celebrations; *Nebuchadnezzar and Semiramis and the creation of the Hanging Gardens of Babylon* finds its counterpart in the work undertaken for the royal estates; *Alexander's Marriage to Roxana* calls to mind the King's marriage; *Cyrus taking arms to rescue a Princess* is a reminder of the war for the Queen's hereditary claims in 1667.

Against the far wall and framing the doors are marble columns and pilasters of the Ionic order. The painted perspectives on the side walls are the work of Jacques Rousseau who also painted the *trompe-l'œil* statues of Meleager and Atalanta between the windows.

An alcove in the middle of the far wall opposite the windows contains the statue of the young Louis XIV, by Jean Warin. Most of the antique busts in this drawing room and the next were part of the original furnishings under the Ancient Regime.

LIGHT MEAL BUFFET FOR COURT EVENINGS AT VERSAILLES
A. TROUVAIN, 1696

MERCURE OF
FRANCE
"Since this
drawing room
is used
to serve the
light supper,
several well-laid
tables line
the walls.
These tables
are covered
with silver
candlesticks
and round,
long and square
filigree baskets.
They are filled
by pyramids
of raw fruit,
lemons, oranges,
all types of dried
and jellied fruits,
and flowers.
Since this food
is to be entirely
consumed,
it remains
uncovered
during the four
hours of
entertainment."

THE DIANA DRAWING ROOM

Louis XIV had initially used this drawing room as a billiards room. In the center stood the billiards table, with a crimson velvet cover fringed with gold. Platforms covered with Persian carpets embroidered in gold and silver were placed around the room for the ladies to sit and watch the game.

The ceiling depicts *Diana in her chariot presiding over hunting and navigation*. The goddess is surrounded by allegories of the nocturnal hours (one reading a book and the other sent to sleep by Cupid showering her with poppies) and the early morning hours spreading flowers and dew. This painting is the work of Gabriel Blanchard, who also executed the monochrome overdoors, each of which evokes an episode from the legend and cult of the goddess of the hunt: *Diana protecting Arethusa*, *A Floral Offering*, and *A Sacrifice to Diana*.

Above the chimney is a painting by Charles de Lafosse depicting *Iphigenia rescued by Diana as she is about to be sacrificed*. A small marble bas-relief of the *Flight to Egypt* is incrusted in the frieze around the chimney; it is attributed to Jacques Sarrazin. On the opposite wall, Gabriel Blanchard painted the Goddess who "forgetting her resolution never to love again, discovers Endymion."

A bust of Louis XIV, sculpted by Bernini in 1685, holds court in the middle of the wall facing the windows. The artist was summoned from Rome to rebuild the Louvre, but this project was never started.

DIANA PRESIDING OVER NAVIGATION AND HUNTING

PRINCESSE PALATINE, VERSAILLES, JANUARY 4, 1699.
"A great debate is underway at court, and everyone from the King down to the lackeys is taking sides. It was Mr. Fagon who raised the question; the Cardinal d'Estrées, Abbé de Vaubran and a few others are on his side; the rest of the court has another opinion. Here is the object of the dispute: does the century start in the year 1700 or in the year 1701?

Mr. Fagon and his party think it should be 1700, because, according to them, one hundred years have passed; but the others argue that the century is only over in the year 1701. I would be interested in knowing Mr. Leibnitz' opinion on this matter. Wherever you go nowadays, you hear people discussing it; even the chairmen talk about it.[…]"

THE SACRIFICE OF IPHIGENIA BY CHARLES DE LAFOSSE

31

THE MARS DRAWING ROOM

The military decor of this room is explained by the fact that it first served as a guard room. It was here that the bodyguards responsible for protecting the monarch were stationed. Under Louis XIV, this room was embellished with a sumptuous suite of silver furniture, which was melted down in 1689 to pay for the League of Augsburg War. It was here that the games took place on evenings when the King held court. A concert or ball would follow, for which the musicians sat in two marble galleries with Ionic columns on either side of the fireplace.

In the center of the ceiling, Mars in a wolf-drawn chariot, painted by Audran, is flanked by Hercules supporting Victory, by Jouvenet, and Terror, Fear and Horror overwhelming the Earthly Powers, by René-Antoine Houasse.

On the walls hang a number of famous paintings, among which are The Pilgrims of Emmaus, in the style of Veronese, and Darius and his family at the feet of Alexander by Charles Le Brun. The painting of David playing the harp, by Domenichino which, at the time of Louis XIV, decorated the alcove in his Chamber, has now been hung over the fireplace. On the side walls hang two magnificent state portraits of Louis XV (by L.M. Van Loo) and Maria Leczinska (by C. Van Loo).

THE MARS
DRAWING ROOM

DAVID PLAYING THE HARP,
BY DOMINICHINO

DUC DE LUYNES, MEMOIRS. "There is no humor in the basic character of the Queen [Marie Leczinska]. She occasionally has moments of vivacity, but they are brief; she is immediately angry about this, and, when she thinks she has hurt someone's feelings, she is anxious to console them with some signs of kindness."

THE CONCERT

A. TROUVAIN

Duc de Luynes, Mémoirs.
"The Queen [Marie Leczinska] should know many things, because she has read a lot, and even books that are difficult to understand, for example the works of P. Mallebranche; she enjoys reading them; however, some people think she may not understand them. Most of her reading, after religious works, is history books. Unfortunately she is not a talented storyteller, and well aware of this; nevertheless, it is easy to see that she is educated."

MARS DRAWN BY WOLVES

THE MERCURY DRAWING ROOM

On evenings when the King held court in this apartment, this drawing room hosted the "King's games".

This room was first used as an antechamber and then as the State Bedchamber. The bed, covered with richly embroidered fabrics and surmounted by a domed canopy, stood at the end of the room, behind a silver balustrade. Everything was melted down in 1689.

On the walls, covered with sumptuous brocades, hung famous paintings, notably by Titian (now in the Louvre).

Over the fireplace hangs a portrait

COUNT OF HÉZECQUES, RECOLLECTIONS OF A PAGE IN LOUIS XVI's COURT.

"In the Mercury Drawing room stood a clock, once very famous, but less so today as such rapid progress has been made in mechanisms. On the hour, roosters would crow and flap their wings. Louis XIV would come out of a temple, and Victory, in a cloud, would crown the monarch as the carillon sounded."

MERCURY DRAWING ROOM

of Louis XV in coronation robes, by Rigaud. A portrait of Maria Leczinska, by Louis Toqué, hangs on the opposite wall. Only one piece of furniture was able to be returned here: the well-known clock presented to Louis XIV by Antoine Morand in 1706. The upper part of the case, of marquetry adorned with gilt chased bronze, is enclosed in glass on all sides, making the mechanism visible to all. At set times, automatons move around a small full-length statue of the King, crowned by a Victory.

The two chests of drawers, the work of Boulle, were delivered to Louis XIV for the Grand Trianon in 1709. The tapestry, depicting the audience granted by the King to the papal nunciate at Fontainebleau in 1664, gives an idea of what a 17th century royal bedchamber was like.

In 1700, the Duc d'Anjou, who became King of Spain, slept in this room.

GILDED STUCCO IN THE SOUTHWEST CEILING CORNER

THE ROYAL FAMILY PLAYING A GAME ON COURT EVENINGS AT VERSAILLES
A. TROUVAIN, 1694

The State of France of 1708
"Every Monday, near eleven thirty in the morning, the footmen set up or have set up a table in the King's antechamber which they cover with a green velvet cloth, and place a chair before the King. Mr. de Chamillart, the Secretary of State, stands to the left of this chair, and after the Council, around twelve thirty, before the King goes to the Chapel to attend Mass, if he hasn't already been, all persons who have petitions to present to the King, come and lay them with respect on this table."

THE APOLLO DRAWING ROOM

This once extraordinarily sumptuous drawing room, the last room of the State Apartment, was also the Throne room.

The wall hangings varied according to the seasons. In winter, they were of crimson velvet with eighteen strips of gold and silver embroidery portraying terms bearing baskets on their heads. In summer, the walls were covered with gold and silver embroidered silk. The throne was placed at the end of the room, on a dais covered with a Persian carpet with a gold background beneath a large canopy. One can still see the three hooks to which the canopy was attached.

The ceiling representing Apollo in his chariot is the work of Charles de Lafosse, a pupil of Le Brun. Since the 18th century, tradition has held that the portrait of Louis XIV by Rigaud should hang opposite the portrait of the reigning King. This is why the portrait of Louis XVI by Callet is across from the portrait of the Sun King over the fireplace, Louis XVI being the last monarch to reside at Versailles. The carved, gilded candelabra were ordered by Louis XV in 1769 for the Hall of Mirrors.

LOUIS XVI
BY CALLET

COUNT OF HÉZECQUES, RECOLLECTIONS OF A PAGE IN LOUIS XVI'S COURT.

"In the first drawing room [...] named after Apollo, was a throne of crimson damask on a dais, but it was never used. The king very rarely held his audiences from atop the throne, at least not from that one. In the same room, a crystal thermometer was attached to the window, and the king would come and check the temperature several times a day. In addition, a footman would record the degrees in his register three times a day."

THE HALL OF MIRRORS

THE WAR
DRAWING ROOM
THE HALL
OF MIRRORS
THE PEACE
DRAWING ROOM

The War Drawing room, along with its counterpart the Peace Drawing room, and the Hall of Mirrors were designed to celebrate the glorious achievements of the one all Europe called King. The paintings in these three rooms, with their historical themes, set them apart from the mythological decor of the State Apartment.

MARQUIS DE DANGEAU, JOURNAL OF LOUIS XIV's COURT.
"The King held an audience for the Ambassadors of Siam, seated on the throne placed for him at the end of the hall which borders the Apartment of Madame la Dauphine.
The ceremony was quite beautiful, and His Majesty said that praise should go to Mr. Aumont, this year's chief lord-in-waiting. The ambassadors spoke quite well; the Abbé de Lyonne, a missionary, acted as their interpreter; they remained at the foot of the throne until they presented the King with the letter from their master; they climbed up to the top step to give it to him. The Siamese then showed profound respect by backing all the way out to the end of the hall, so as not to turn their backs on the King.
There are three ambassadors; they are accompanied by four gentlemen and two secretaries; the rest of their entourage is of no importance. "

BARBIER, JOURNAL, JULY 1722
" It is obvious that the King [Louis XV, then a child] is very happy to be at Versailles. Upon arriving, he went to the Chapel where the Holy Sacrament is displayed and prayed to. From there, and despite the heat, he toured the shady gardens; he then returned to the Hall and sat directly on the parquet floor. Everyone followed suit. The Prince Regent had to borrow a shirt to change, because his apartment was not yet furnished. However, this place is much more fit for a King than Paris."

THE WAR DRAWING ROOM

Mansart began work on the War Drawing room in 1678. Its decor, completed by Le Brun in 1686, celebrates the military victories which led to the Peace Treaty of Nimeguen.

The walls are lined with marble panels adorned with six gilt-bronze trophies and cascades of weapons. On the wall adjacent to the Apollo Drawing room is a huge oval stucco bas-relief of Louis XIV on horseback riding in triumph over his enemies. This masterpiece by Coysevox is surmounted by two gilt figures representing Fame, and held up by two gilt prisoners bound with chains of flowers. Below, on a bas-relief set into a false fireplace, Clio writes the King's history for posterity.

The ceiling was painted by Le Brun and depicts *France in arms seated on a cloud surrounded by Victories.*

Her shield is ornamented with a portrait of Louis XIV. The coves contain the three conquered enemies: Germany, on her knees, with her eagle; Spain, threatening, with her roaring lion; Holland, lying on her lion; as well as *Bellona, Goddess of War, raging with anger between Rebellion and Discord.*

WAR DRAWING ROOM OPENING ON THE HALL OF MIRRORS

THE HALL OF MIRRORS

Originally, this was simply a terrace which Le Vau had built to surround Louis XIII's small château.

But in 1678, the architect Hardouin-Mansart replaced it with a hall to link the King's apartment to those of the Queen. Scores of decorators worked under the direction of Le Brun from 1679 to 1686. The Hall of Mirrors receives abundant light from the gardens and the park through seventeen large, arched windows. They are reflected in the bevelled mirrors of seventeen simulated arcades. The ceiling paintings recount the most important events in the personal reign of Louis XIV, from 1661 to 1678. The furnishings that now decorate the Hall of Mirrors are replicas of the decor used during the marriage of the Dauphin (the future Louis XVI) to Marie-Antoinette in 1770; twenty-four candelabra were molded from original models now in the Museum of Versailles. Twenty chandeliers of silvered bronze, adorned with Bohemian crystal, are a reminder of the lighting in the Hall of Mirrors for official festivities or masked balls during the Ancient Regime.

CANDELABRA IN THE HALL OF MIRRORS

THE HALL OF MIRRORS

The Hall of Mirrors was used above all as a passageway from the King's Apartment to those of the Queen. One thus avoided the King's Bedchamber by going through the Bull's Eye Drawing room or Council Chamber. Every day the courtiers would stand in attendance here as the King and the Royal Family went by on their way to and from Mass. But it was also used for receptions on exceptional occasions: the King granted a state audience to the Doge of Genoa in 1685, the Ambassadors of Siam in 1686, the Persian Ambassadors in 1715. Louis XV and Louis XVI followed the tradition of these state audiences. It was here, too, that the illuminations were lit and masked balls were held for marriages of princes of the Royal Family.

After the Ancient Regime, the Hall of Mirrors again became the setting for important events. On January 18, 1871, the King of Prussia solemnly accepted his crown as Emperor of Germany. And on June 28, 1919, the Hall was the site of the signing of the Treaty of Versailles that put an end to World War I.

THE DOGE OF GENOA MAKING AMENDS TO LOUIS XIV IN THE HALL OF MIRRORS AT VERSAILLES, MAY 15, 1685

CENTRAL PART OF THE HALL OF MIRRORS CEILING "THE KING RULES BY HIMSELF"
CHARLES LE BRUN

MERCURE DE FRANCE, REPORT OF THE RECEPTION OF THE DOGE OF GENOA, ON THE 15TH MAY 1685. "After climbing the superb staircase leading to His Majesty's state apartment, one entered the War Drawing room, which is at the end and joins the hall, and from this drawing room one turned into the hall, at the end of which was the King, in the drawing room [Peace Drawing room] which is directly opposite the one we had just passed through. Two things stood out: one was that this apartment and this hall were beautifully furnished, with several millions worth of silver wares; the other was the tremendous crowd everywhere, although these apartments and this hall together could contain as many people as found in the largest palace. Despite the orders given to clear way along the hall, the Doge had trouble passing through. Field-marshal Duc de Duras, Captain of the Palace bodyguards, who had greeted him at the entrance of the guard room, accompanied him to His Majesty's throne. It was made of silver, and on two raised platforms. Mgr the Dauphin (the Crown Prince) and Monsieur (the King's brother) were next to the King. His Majesty was surrounded by all the Royal Princes, and by his chief officers who held special positions near him during such ceremonies. The Doge's entourage was quite large, most of them being unable to follow him up to the throne, and they took up the empty space in middle of the hall, which had been cleared to make way for him. As soon as the Doge saw the King and realized he could be recognized, he took his hat off. He took a few more steps forward and then made, along with his Senators, two deep bows to His Majesty. The King stood up, and answered these bows by slightly raising his hat; after which the monarch motioned to them to approach him, as if extending his hand. The Doge then stood on the first step of the throne and made a third bow, as well as his four Senators. The King and the Doge then replaced their hats. All the princes did likewise, but the four Senators remained bare-headed."

**AUDIENCE
GRANTED BY
LOUIS XIV TO
THE PERSIAN
AMBASSADOR
AT VERSAILLES,
FEBRUARY 19,
1715**

LE MERCURE GALANT,
ACCOUNT OF
THE PARTY GIVEN BY
THE KING FOR
NEW YEAR'S 1708.
"Seventy-two guards from H.M.'s Swiss guards company were chosen to carry the platters, and since mass confusion would easily reign, if each did not know to which table he was to bring the platters he was in charge of, these four troops were each assigned different colored ribbons that corresponded to each table, making it impossible for one troop to mix with those of another, as long as they stayed with those who wore ribbons of the same color. Several of the King's controllers had been appointed to bring the meats; there were to be two per table. [_] Whenever a queen raised her glass, we respected the old tradition, and calls of "the Queen drinks" rang out in chorus; and since two or three queens sometimes drank at the same time, the noise from these calls was more or less loud, but always quite pleasant; the ladies' voices were usually above that of the men who were at these tables [_] some clapped their hands, others found a way to harmoniously strike some piece of silver, and all these noises and the way they came from different tones were in a way entertaining and greatly contributed to the day's ceremony."

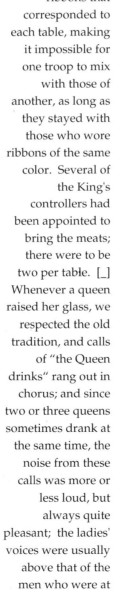

THE PEACE DRAWING ROOM

Situated at the south end of the Hall of Mirrors, the Peace Drawing room is the counterpart of the War Drawing room particularly by virtue of its decor of marble, mirrors and gilt bronze. The ceiling is by Le Brun. In the center, one sees *France crossing the skies in a chariot drawn by four doves, preceded by Peace, crowned by Glory with the halo of Immortality and accompanied by Hymen, while Magnificence shows her the plans of the buildings to be erected.* In the coves are *Spain, Christian Europe at Peace, Germany and Holland.* Above the marble fireplace is an oval painting by Lemoine in 1729. It portrays *Louis XV bestowing peace on Europe.*

In 1710, this drawing room was annexed to the Queen's Apartment as a Games room.

FÉLIBIEN, ACCOUNT OF THE PARTY HELD AT VERSAILLES ON JULY 18, 1668. "Having granted peace at the request of his allies and of all Europe, and shown signs of unparalleled moderation and justice, even in the greatest of his conquests, the King was now only interested in ruling his kingdom when, to compensate for what the Court had missed during carnival in his absence, he decided to organize a gala in the gardens of Versailles where, in spite of the pleasures offered by such a delightful setting, the mind nonetheless marveled at the surprising, extraordinary beauty with which this great prince so deftly spices all his festivities."

PEACE DRAWING ROOM: "LOUIS XV BESTOWING PEACE ON EUROPE"

PAINTED BY LEMOINE

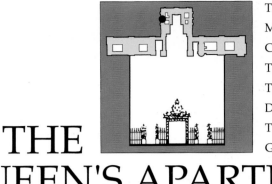

THE QUEEN'S BEDCHAMBER
MARIE-ANTOINETTE'S
CABINETS
THE PEERS' ROOM
THE GRAND COUVERT
DINING ROOM
THE QUEEN'S
GUARD ROOM

THE QUEEN'S APARTMENT

The Queen's Apartment, with its different rooms overlooking the South Parterre, runs parallel to the King's State Apartment. It was altered several times until the end of the Ancient Regime. This apartment consists of five rooms: the Guard Room (which opens on to the Marble Stairway called the Queen's Staircase), the Grand Couvert antechamber, the Peers' Room, the Queen's Bedchamber and the Peace Drawing room.

LOUIS XIV, MEMOIRS FOR THE INSTRUCTION OF THE CROWN PRINCE "You were born, my son, on the first of November. As all these things that bring glory upon my Kingdom and myself had just been accomplished or appeared well advanced, I took it as a secret sign that Heaven did not destine you to shame your country. The joy of my subjects, which was great at your birth, revealed to me what natural affection they bear their princes, and yet forebode all they would expect of you one day, all they would eternally reproach you with, my son, should you not meet those expectations."

PARTIAL VIEW OF THE QUEEN'S BEDCHAMBER IN 1993

THE QUEEN'S APARTMENT

The Queen's Bedchamber was the main room in her apartment. It was here that, each morning after her toilette, she would grant her private audiences. This room is also where she would give birth to the Heir to the Throne.

This bedchamber was first occupied by Queen Marie-Thérèse; its appearance was altered several times, between 1729 and 1735 for Marie Leczinska, and from 1770 to 1782 for Marie-Antoinette.

The room has been recreated as it was on October 6, 1789 when Marie-Antoinette left the palace for the last time. Its summer furnishings were reconstituted from models of the silks, trimmings and embroidery made in 1787.

To the left of the bed stands the jewelry cabinet made by Schwerdfegger, and given to the Queen in 1787.

CEILING MEDAILLON : "THE QUEEN'S VIRTUES"
BY BOUCHER

DUC DE LUYNES, MÉMOIRS. "Yesterday morning began the re-upholstering of the Queen's bedchamber; complete summer suite with bed, tapestries, armchairs, folding screens, door curtains. There are only two armchairs; no more are placed in the Queen's bedchamber. The fabric is from Tours, white, embroidered and painted. The bed and curtains are beautiful and pleasant to the eye. In the center of each tapestry panel is a large vase, which is striking; but the ornaments that go with it are all off-center as is the new fashion."

THE QUEEN'S BEDCHAMBER

MARIE-ANTOINETTE'S CABINETS

The Queen's Private Cabinets served varying purposes under each Queen: Marie-Thérèse of Austria had an oratory created, whereas Maria Leczinska and Marie-Antoinette were able to decorate these rooms more to their taste than their State Apartment.

The Cabinets, today as they were left by Marie-Antoinette, comprise essentially a bathroom and its retiring chamber, two libraries, a drawing room and a boudoir.

The boudoir, also called the "Meridian Cabinet", was used by the Queen to rest at midday. The present decor was created on the birth of the first Dauphin in 1781, but the chairs were not delivered until 1784.

Formerly, the Duchess de Bourgogne had an oratory here, then it became a small drawing room for Maria Leczinska and, finally, a staircase.

A bathroom and its retiring chamber bear witness to the refined comfort which, despite what one may think, existed at Versailles in the 18th century.

The Private Cabinet, which had previously been used as a drawing room by Maria Leczinska, was entirely redecorated in 1783 in the style of antiquity. The Queen's architect, Mique, designed the wood panelling carved by the Rousseau brothers; it depicts sphinxes back to back against an incense burner on a tripod. The red griotte marble fireplace is embellished with gilt bronzes and figures of female caryatids. Opposite the windows is an alcove lined with mirrors. All the furniture once belonged to

Marie-Antoinette, but was not necessarily in this room. It was in this room that Marie-Antoinette frequently received not only her favorite painter, Mrs Vigée-Lebrun, but also her former music teacher, Gluck, of whom she was the patroness, and her appointed milliner, Miss Bertin. During the previous reign, Maria Leczinska would meet with her friends here, such as President Menardt, who described these meetings in his memoirs.

On the mezzanine above the Queen's Private Cabinets, small rooms have recently been restored as they were before the Revolution. This apartment, where the Queen lived her private life, includes a drawing room (redecorated with its original silks) which served as a billiards room until 1783, a dining room, and the chambermaids' quarters.

"MARIE-ANTOINETTE POSING FOR THE ARTIST IN HER BEDCHAMBER AT VERSAILLES"
JEAN-BAPTISTE ANDRÉ GAUTIER-DAGOTY

"QUEEN MARIE-ANTOINETTE IN RIDING CLOTHES"
ADOLF ULRICH WERTMULLER

MARIE-
ANTOINETTE'S
BILLIARDS
CABINET
BECAME A
SITTING ROOM
FOR THE UPPER
STOREY OF
CABINETS
IN 1787

MADAME CAMPAN,
MEMOIRS.
"The mistress of the robes was responsible for ordering the fabric, the dresses, the Court regalia; of settling and paying the accounts; everything was submitted to her and was only discharged upon her signature and at her order, from the slippers to the embroidered clothing from Lyon. [_] She also had under her orders an assistant mistress of the robes responsible for taking care of the Queen's clothing; two women to fold and iron objects that required such care; two valets of the robes and a groom of the robes who was responsible for conveying to her apartments, every morning, baskets covered with taffeta which contained everything the Queen was to wear throughout the day, and large dressing cases of green taffeta that enveloped the clothing and dresses. Every morning, the valet of the robes on duty presented to the mistress a book which held samples of the robes, court gowns, day dresses, etc. A small portion of the trimming indicated what type it was; the mistress presented this book, when the Queen awoke, along with a pincushion; Her Majesty marked with a pin all she wished to wear that day: one for the court gown she wanted, one for the day dress for the afternoon, one for the dress gown for gaming or dinner in the private apartments. This book was taken back to the wardrobe, and soon would arrive the large taffeta cases containing everything needed for the entire day."

THE PEERS' ROOM

This drawing room was where the Queen held her audiences. It runs parallel to the Throne room and the King's second antechamber.

All that remains of the decor carried out under Le Brun for Queen Marie-Thérèse is the ceiling painted in 1671 by Michel Corneille. This work is inspired by the arts and sciences as practised by celebrated female figures of classical mythology.

When Marie-Antoinette's second son, the Duc de Normandie and future Louis XVII, was born, the Queen asked her architect, Mique, to redecorate the room entirely. The marble and stucco were replaced by waist-high wainscotting, and the walls covered with hangings of apple-green silk, gallooned with gold. Mirrors and a slate-blue marble fireplace adorned with chased bronze by Gouthière completed the decor. The console tables and corner cupboards by Riesener, as well as the tapestry of Louis XV, were also installed at that time.

"MERCURY SPREADING HIS INFLUENCE OVER THE ARTS" CENTRAL CEILING DECOR

THE PEERS' ROOM

THE GRAND COUVERT DINING ROOM

This room is called the Grand Couvert Dining room for it was here that, in the 18th century, the King and Queen ate in public. However, it is also referred to as the Queen's Antechamber, for it was here that the visitors who had come from the Queen's Guard room would wait to be brought before Her Majesty, either in the Peers' Room or in her Bedchamber. This room also served as a theater. In 1671, a small removable theater was created here. Later, Marie-Antoinette had a musicians' gallery built on the east wall, and on ball evenings, a false ceiling covered the original one. The lower part of the walls is lined with marble panels, and a cornice with gilded consoles and small trophies runs along the top. In the corners are large gilded trophies surmounted with cupids. The central ceiling painting, by Claude Vignon, has disappeared and been replaced by an old replica of Darius' Tent, by Le Brun. However, several other paintings by Vignon still remain on the archings.

"MARIE-ANTOINETTE AND HER CHILDREN"
BY MME VIGÉE-LEBRUN

THE QUEEN'S GRAND COUVERT ANTECHAMBER

THE QUEEN'S GUARD ROOM

Up until 1676, this site was occupied by the galleries of the chapel. When it was transferred to the adjoining room, a floor was laid and the walls covered with marble panels. In 1680, it became the new Queen's Guard room.

The overdoors are embellished with gilt metal bas-reliefs by Le Gros and Massou. The painted decor is the work of Noël Coypel who had originally made the five large ceiling paintings for the Jupiter Drawing room (situated on the site of the current War Drawing room). A *trompe-l'œil* frieze is painted in the corners of the ceiling, and courtiers of Louis XIV can be seen leaning on the false railing. Two more of the artist's paintings illustrate other aspects of the story of Jupiter: over the fireplace *Sacrifice to the Ruler of Olympus* and, on the opposite wall *The Corybants dancing to prevent the cries of young Jupiter from reaching Saturn*. A door to the right of the chimney leads to the Queen's Private Cabinets.

CON SIGNE
DE LA SENTINELLE DE LA REINE

La sentinelle de la Salle de la Reine, ne laissera passer aucun prêtre ni moine inconnu sans un billet du Capitaine, même avec un billet du Capitaine, il ne les les laissera point entrer au grand couvert à moins d'un ordre exprès.

Il ne laissera passer aucune autre personne inconnue, de mauvaise mine ou nouvellement marquée de la Petite Vérolle.

Il ne restera dans la Salle d'autres chaisses à porteurs, que celles de la Famille Royalle, des Princes et Princesses du Sang.

Il n'y souffrira rester aucun homme de Livrée.

La livrée des Princes et Princesses du Sang, du Chevalier d'honneur Dᵃᵉ d'honᵉ et d'Atours, dit grand Aumonier de la Reine, passeront dans l'antichambre.

Il laissera passer un Seul domestique, des Cardinaux et des Ministres,

THE CORONATION ROOM

This room, which follows the Queen's State Apartment, is named after the painting of the Coronation of Napoleon I, by David, which Louis-Philippe had placed here. From 1676 to 1682, the château's third chapel occupied the site, which later became the Great Guard room. It was there that, each Maundy Thursday, the ceremony commemorating the Last Supper took place, and the King of France would kneel to wash the feet of thirteen poor children. In 1732, 1771 and 1787, Louis XV and Louis XVI held special sessions of the Parliament in this room. Since the reign of Louis-Philippe, three large works decorate this room. The two paintings by David *The Coronation of the Emperor* and *The Distribution of Eagle Standards on the Champ-de-Mars* were commissioned by Napoleon I. And the third, *The Battle of Aboukir*, opposite the windows, was commissioned by Murat from the painter Gros. The overdoors are embellished with figures of Courage, Genius, Generosity and Constance, the work of Gérard. The ceiling depicts an allegorical painting by Callet of the *18th Brumaire*. In the center of the room stands a bronze and Sèvres porcelain column commissioned by Napoleon to commemorate the battle of Austerlitz.

COMTE D'HÉZECQUES, RECOLLECTIONS OF A PAGE IN LOUIS XVI's COURT.

"This ceremony [of the Last Supper], sanctioned by an ancient custom and by the example of God in person, was a touching sight set against the contrast of power and humility, the master serving the subjects. […] On the morning of Maundy Thursday, twelve young children were lined up in the main Guard room, their freshness equal to that of the enormous bouquet of the rarest flowers they held in their hands. […] The ceremony began at nine o'clock with a sermon. On that day, the preacher could voice all the vehemence of his zeal and thunder loudly against the abuses and scandals of the court. […] Each child held his right foot over a vermeil basin held by a chaplain; the Comte d'Artois poured a few drops of water over it; Monsieur wiped it with the towel the child wore around his neck, and the king kissed the foot."

THE 1792 ROOM

The 1792 Room was once used as a passage from the Great Guard room, now the Coronation Room, to the Princes' Staircase and the South Wing. Called the Room of the Merchants under Louis XV, this room became the Swiss Guards room during the reign of Louis XVI. The paintings decorating it depict the 1792 campaign.

THE CORONATION OF NAPOLEON I
BY DAVID

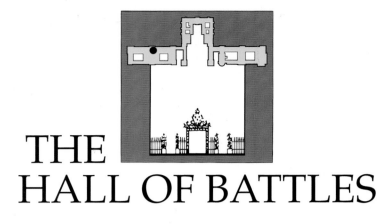

THE HALL OF BATTLES

The Princes' Wing, called the South Wing, was built by Jules Hardouin-Mansart between 1678 and 1682.

While its external appearance has been preserved, this is not the case of the interior. There were fourteen apartments in the attic storey which could be subdivided, and five large apartments on the first floor. The ground floor and first floor apartments opened onto halls which led through archways on the east to interior courtyards and were linked by several stairways, including two large ones at each end of the wing, the Provence and Princes' Staircases.

Under Louis-Philippe's reign, this site was chosen for the installation of the Hall of Battles. This Hall, 394 feet long and 43 feet wide, fills the entire length of the South Wing's first floor. It is now a gallery containing a collection of large paintings portraying the great military events of French history. The architects, Fontaine and Nepveu, designed a solemn decor to match the serious subject matter. The paintings cover 14 centuries of French history, from the Battle of Tolbiac, fought by Clovis in 496, to that of Wagram, which Napoleon won in 1809.

THE HALL
OF BATTLES

EZÉCHIEL SPANHEIM, ACCOUNT OF EVENTS AT THE FRENCH COURT IN 1690. "The Court of France, given its position under this reign, is exceedingly obedient to its king, so that there is great haste to prove one's fervor and court him, and equal devotion to carrying out, with total and precise regularity, the duties each person is called upon to perform. […] So that all the courtiers, down to the lowliest, strive to see the King and be seen by him on every occasion that arises."

YOUNG LOUIS XIV

BY LE BRUN

LOGGIA OF THE QUEEN'S STAIRCASE

THE KING'S APARTMENT

THE QUEEN'S STAIRCASE
THE KING'S BEDCHAMBER
THE COUNCIL CHAMBER

Unlike the State Apartment, which was mostly used for receptions, the King's Apartment consisted of the rooms effectively lived in by the sovereign; it was there that the various daily ceremonies dictated by *etiquette* took place.

After the loggia of the Queen's Staircase, one crosses the Guard room and the First Antechamber or *Grand Couvert* Antechamber, whose simple painted decor dates from 1692.

Then comes the Second Antechamber, called the Bull's Eye Antechamber, after the oval windows in the large cornice decorated with children at play. It was in this large room, which was given its present size and decor in 1701, that the courtiers would wait each day behind the door leading to the King's Bedchamber until it was time for the sovereign's Rising and Retiring Ceremonies.

THE STATE OF FRANCE IN 1708.

"It is the custom to make the King's bed while His Majesty attends Mass. To make it, a valet stands on either side, with a servant at the foot. One of the valets on duty must guard the King's bed throughout the day, [...] When the King leaves the château of Versailles for several days, a valet remains behind to guard the bed, and sleeps at the foot of His Majesty's bed. "

COMTE D'HÉZECQUES, RECOLLECTIONS OF A PAGE IN LOUIS XVI'S COURT.

" Eight guards from the Scots company were designated guards of the sleeve; in fact, when in public, two of them, on service every day, never strayed from the king's sleeve. Their duty was to keep constant watch over the king; and it can be said that only the closing of his casket would signal the end of their responsibility, since it was up to them to place the body in the casket and escort it to Saint-Denis. They wore haquetons over their uniforms, a type of tunic covered with silver and gold embroidery in a brush pattern."

**GUARDS OF
THE SLEEVE AT
THE CHATEAU
OF VERSAILLES
UNDER
LOUIS XV**

THE QUEEN'S STAIRCASE

The first staircase, erected in 1672 and also of marble, was replaced in 1681 by the larger one we can now visit. The work was undertaken to make an equal counterpart to the newly completed staircase leading to the King's Apartment.

The large trompe-l'œil painting is by Meusnier, for the architecture, Pœrson, for the characters and Belin de Fontenay, for the flowers. The "gilt metal" bas-reliefs of the overdoors were made by Le Gros and Massou.

THE KING'S BEDCHAMBER

This room, part of Louis XIII's small château, was first the State Drawing room that separated the King's Private Apartment from those of the Queen. Then, in 1684, it became the King's dressing room. It was not until 1701 that Louis XIV decided to make this his bedchamber.

When the Hall of Mirrors was built in 1678, the windows overlooking the gardens were removed and the entire decor was altered the following year.

In 1701, the alcove was built and Nicolas Coustou made the gilded carving above the bed, *France watching over the King in his slumber.* Louis XIV died in this bedchamber on September 1, 1715.

After 1738, the room was used only for the "Rising" and "Retiring" ceremonies. The room has been recreated as it was in the summers from 1722 to 1785.

THE KING'S
BEDCHAMBER

First nominations of the Knights of the Order of Saint-Louis by Louis XIV at Versailles on May 10, 1693

Saint-Simon, Memoirs.
"At eight o'clock, the head valet on duty, who was the only one to sleep in the King's Bedchamber, and who was dressed, awakened him. The chief physician and the chief surgeon, along with the king's nurse until she passed away, entered at the same time. She went to kiss him, the others rubbed him, and often changed his nightshirt, as he was subject to sweating. After fifteen minutes, the grand chamberlain was called, or in his absence the chief lord-in-waiting of the year, and with them the main officials. One of the two opened the curtains which were closed, and presented holy water from the holy basin near the bed. These gentlemen remained there a moment, and one of them spoke to the King if they had something to tell him or to ask, and then the others moved off. When none had anything to say, they remained only a few moments. The one who opened the curtains and presented the holy water also presented the Book of the Office of the Holy Spirit, then all went into the Council Chambers. Once this short service ended, the King called out and they returned. The same one gave him his dressing gown. [...] As soon as he was dressed, he went to pray to God at the foot of his bed and all the clergy got down on their knees, even the cardinals; all the laymen remained standing, and the Captain of the Guards came to the balustrade during the prayer, after which the King went to his cabinet. There he found, or was followed by, everyone entitled to enter, who were varied in their offices. He gave orders to each for the day, and so it was known to within a quarter hour all that the King intended to do. Afterward everyone left. The only ones to remain were the bastards, Mr. de Montchevreuil and Mr. d'O, as well as their tutors, Mansart and after him d'Antin, all of whom entered not by the bedchamber but from the hall behind, and the house valets. That was leisure for one and all, a time for discussing the plans for the gardens and the buildings, and it lasted until the King had to tend to affairs."

Saint-Simon, Memoirs.
"Supper was always intimate, that is to say taken alone in his bedchamber, on a square table across from the central window. It was more or less

substantial; for in the morning he ordered a small or very small supper. But even the latter included many dishes, and three courses without the fruit. Once the table had been set, the main courtiers entered, then all who were known, and the chief lord-in-waiting of the year went to call the King. He served him if the grand chamberlain was absent. […] I have seen, although very rarely, Monseigneur and his sons stand through an intimate supper, without the King ever offering them a seat. I have constantly seen princes and cardinals standing in a row. I have often seen Monsieur, either coming from Saint-Cloud to see the King, or leaving the Council of Dispatches, the only one he entered. He handed over the briefcase and remained standing. A bit later, the King, noting he hadn't left, asked him if he wouldn't like to sit down; he bowed, and the King ordered that a seat be brought for him. A stool was placed behind him. A few moments later, the King told him, "Please do be seated, Brother."

THE COUNCIL CHAMBER

This site was formerly occupied by two rooms: the King's Cabinet where he held his various councils with his Ministers, and the Cabinet of Terms, also called the Cabinet of Periwigs (the King's wigs were kept in a wardrobe in this room). In 1755, Louis XV ordered his architect, Jacques-Ange Gabriel, to make the two rooms into one. The ministerial council was held here regularly and it was here that all the important decisions of the reigns of Louis XV and Louis XVI were made. The King also granted private audiences in this room.

THE COUNCIL
CHAMBER

THE KING'S PRIVATE APARTMENT

During the reign of Louis XIV, the King's private apartment consisted of a series of drawing rooms and cabinets which, with the exception of the billiards room, formed a veritable private museum. Only rare guests of honor, scholars and artists were admitted to contemplate the masterpieces of the royal collections.

In 1738, when Louis XV had a small bedchamber created for himself here, the private apartment was reorganized to include a first antechamber (Cabinet of the Dogs), second antechamber (Clock Cabinet) and study (Private Cabinet).

LA MARTINIERE, MÉMOIRES.

"In the back of the room, opposite the doors and windows, is a deep-set alcove that holds the bed. This alcove opens between two pilasters, at each side corner of which palm trees rise up, bend in an arch and extend along the top rail; this rail is curved, and the King's coat of arms is carved in the middle. This alcove is enclosed by a richly decorated balustrade. The wall hangings are made of superb fabrics, and match those of the bed.

The rest of the room is decorated with wainscotting, that goes up to the cornice. When coming from the Council Chamber, you can see a fireplace in the middle of this wainscotting, it is made of beautiful breccia marble from Alep; its shape is modern and graceful, with decorations carved out of the marble itself. Above this is a mirrored glass panel, surrounded a peculiar carved frame. On the opposite side is a similar panel. The walls on the window side are also lined with mirrors. The pilasters and the panels vary in several parts with very tasteful decorations. The cornice around the ceiling is slightly curved and forms a frame, with middle and corner pieces, and profiles, in which various types of cartouches are set, which enclose monograms and small bas-reliefs matching the other decorations.

On each of the four doors, two of which are on either side of the fireplace, and two next to the mirrored panel on the opposite side, are paintings enclosed in sumptuous frames: one is the portrait of François I by Titian, the second is Catherine de Medecis by Rubens; another, Marie de Medicis by Van Dyck; the last is the portrait of Don Juan of Austria by Antoine Moro. The King usually sleeps in this bedchamber; and when he wakes in the morning, either he goes into the Council Chamber in his dressing gown, or rises according to the accustomed ceremonies."

LOUIS XV'S BEDCHAMBER

In Louis XV's bedchamber, the alcove, once enclosed by a gilt balustrade, is covered with a gold embroidered lampas fabric, a reproduction of Louis XIV's last "summer" decor.

The overdoors hold portraits of Louis XV's daughters, Mesdames Elisabeth, Henriette and Adelaïde by the school of Nattier; they replaced the paintings by Titian, Antonio Moro, Rubens and Van Dyck that used to be in this room.

Louis XV died in this room on May 10, 1774.

THE CLOCK CABINET

Louis XV had the two rooms originally here made into one in 1738. In 1760, the famous astronomical clock by Passement, Dauthiau and Caffieri was placed here, followed, in 1775, by the splendid barometer by Lemaire and Mazière.

COMTE D'HÉZECQUES, RECOLLECTIONS OF A PAGE IN LOUIS XVI's COURT. "In the King's private apartment which I have already mentioned, stood, by day, the valets and the valets of the robes on duty at the château; but the fourth room, called Large Cabinet, was where the head valet stayed. In the middle, one could see the reduced model of the bronze statue standing in Louis XV Square, and the famous Passement clock, seven feet high, that not only displayed the hours, years, months, etc. but indicated the lunar phases and revolutions of the planets. And on New Year's eve, the King always stayed up past midnight to watch his clock change completely."

THE CLOCK CABINET

PORTRAIT OF LOUIS XV BY VINCENT DE MONTPETIT

THE CABINET OF THE DOGS

First ante-chamber of the King's Private Apartment, it was created in 1738. To decorate this room, Gabriel used the wainscotting previously in Louis XIV's former billiards room. Its name comes from the kennels placed along the walls for Louis XV's favorite dogs.

AFTER-HUNT DINING ROOM

The room was created in 1750 on the site of Louis XV's former bathroom. This is where the King used to dine with some of the people who had taken part in the hunt.

MARQUIS D'ARGENSON, JOURNAL. "The King's [Louis XV] dogs really lead a dog's life; at the beginning of the year, he makes plans for what his animals will do until the end. He has five or six packs of dogs whose hunting, resting, and walking characteristics must be combined. I'm not just talking about mixing and handling old and young dogs, of their names and qualities, which the King knows better than anyone in his kennels, but of arranging these schedules, according to the planned and to-be-planned trips; this is done using maps, a combined calendar, and some say that His Majesty manages the finances and runs his wars with less attention than he does all this."

BAROMETER BY SCULPTOR JEAN-JOSEPH LEMAIRE IN THE CLOCK CABINET

THE KING'S PRIVATE CABINET

It was not until 1753 that this room became the King's Study. Prior to that it had been Louis XIV's Picture Gallery; it was connected to the adjoining rooms by two arcades. In 1738, Louis XV had the arcades removed and a fireplace of Italian griotte marble installed. At the same time, the King commissioned the cabinet maker Gaudreaux to make a medals chest-of-drawers decorated with magnificent gilt bronzes.

In 1753, the walls were lined with wainscotting designed by Gabriel and carved by Verberckt. Two years later the cabinet maker Joubert delivered two corner cupboards to match the medals chest. Then in 1760, Louis XV commissioned from Oeben the famous rolltop writing desk in the center of the room, it was eventually completed in 1769 by Reisener.

The "American Independence" candelabrum and two accompanying vases date from the time of Louis XVI.

The crimson damask gallooned with gold was re-woven for the drapes and the chairs by Foliot, delivered in 1774, making this room one of the most fully restored in the château.

Behind the Study is the Arrière Cabinet in which both Louis XV and Louis XVI actually worked, as seen by the shelving used to store their files.

MEDAL CHEST MADE BY GAUDREAUX

ROLL-TOP WRITTING DESK IN THE KING'S PRIVATE CABINET

THE NEW ROOMS

This is a suite of rooms which Louis XV had created on the site of a small gallery constructed in 1684 to replace Madame de Montespan's apartment. It had five windows looking on to the Royal Courtyard and a drawing room at each end. The ceilings were painted by Mignard.

In 1752, the entire suite was demolished so that Louis XV's daughter, Madame Adélaïde, could live near him. The Princess lived here until 1769, when the rooms which had made up her apartment were integrated into the King's Private Suite and called the "New Rooms".

The first room is called the Cabinet of the Gold Plate; it used to be Madame Adélaïde's Private Cabinet. Beyond this lies Louis XV's former bathroom, transformed for Louis XVI into his très arrière cabinet or Room 174 of the Privy Purse.

Next is the library, created on Louis XVI's accession in 1774. It is the last work by the architect Jacques-Ange Gabriel.

Then comes the dining room, formerly Madame Adélaïde's State Cabinet, referred to as the "Porcelain dining room" during Louis XIV's reign. Each year at Christmas the latest pieces produced by the Sèvres Porcelain Factory were exhibited here.

Beyond lies a room redecorated in the 19th century, the former Billiards Room, which was also used as a Buffet Room. Louis XVI's Games Room, dating from 1775, brings the King's Private Apartment to a close. It had previously been Louis XIV's Cabinet of Curios and Rare Objects, and then Madame Adélaïde's first antechamber. The wainscotting has been restored and the fireplace, removed in the 19th century, has been replaced. In addition, a large part of the original furnishings have been found and returned to this room.

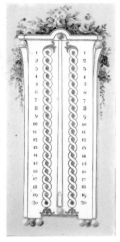

BILLIARDS SCOREBOARD, DECORATED BY THE PAINTER LEVE IN 1786

THE CABINET OF THE GOLD PLATE

LOUIS XVI'S LIBRARY

THE PORCELAIN DINING ROOM

LOUIS XVI'S GAMES ROOM

THE KING'S PRIVATE CABINETS

The King's Private Cabinets (built during the reign of Louis XV) are situated under the château's roofs, directly above the King's State Apartment and on different levels. They overlook the Marble Courtyard and several inner courtyards.

These rooms were originally allocated to the King's courtiers and servants. As these rooms could be easily reached from his apartment by means of inner stairways, Louis XV found it convenient to convert them into relaxation and leisure cabinets (library, physics and chemistry cabinets, aviaries, bathroom, small dining room, etc.) He also had an apartment assigned to his latest mistress, from Madame de Mailly up to the last, Madame du Barry.

After Louis XV died, Louis XVI banished Madame du Barry from Court and gave this apartment to his minister Maurepas and to the Duc de Villequier, the chief lord-in-waiting. But just like his grandfather, he kept various studies for himself in the remaining rooms.

Madame de Pompadour once had an apartment located above the Mercury and Apollo Drawing rooms on the garden side; seeing this arrangement, it is easy to imagine what some of the courtesans' apartments were like during the Ancient Regime.

THE STATE CABINET

DUC DE LUYNES, MEMOIRS
"The King [Louis XV] loves women, and yet there is no gallantry in his spirit; it can even be said that he is stony in character. Details on illnesses, operations, often things regarding anatomy, questions on where to be buried, are unfortunately common subjects of conversation; even the ladies are not spared such questions. He always seems to view with pessimism the diseases related to him […]"

THE THEATER

Up until the construction of the present Royal Opera, several temporary theaters had been erected at Versailles. In 1700, one of these was created in the vestibule of the Prince's Courtyard. Another theater was created at the time of Madame de Pompadour, first in the Small Gallery and later in the Ambassadors' Staircase. Great festivities were also held on the grounds of the Great Stables.

THE ROYAL OPERA

In 1685, a project presented by the Italian stage setter, Vigarani (on the site of the present Opera), was interrupted by the wars which marked the end of Louis XIV's reign. It wasn't until 1748 that Louis XV decided to provide the château with a theater, and commissioned his Head Architect, Jacques-Ange Gabriel, to draw up the plans. Gabriel worked for 20 years on the project, continually altering and improving his plans. The Seven Years' War brought a halt to the initial work. Gabriel was about to give up when Louis XV suddenly ordered the building to be completed in 21 months for the marriage of his grandson, the Dauphin and future Louis XVI, to the Archduchess Marie-Antoinette.

The theater was intended not only for operas but also for concerts, balls and banquets. Gabriel designed an elliptical ground plan, and for acoustic as well as financial reasons, the theater was built entirely of wood, painted to look like marble. With the help of the stage setter, Arnoult, who advised him on the design of the stage, Gabriel created a decor of solid wood with boxes and tiers matching those in the theater itself.

The banquet held here in 1789 for the officers of the King's Bodyguard brought the celebrations of the Ancient Regime to a riotous close.

The Theater was not reopened until the inaugural celebrations for the Museum during Louis-Philippe's reign. Restoration work undertaken on this occasion considerably altered the decor of the theater; however, it was restored to its former appearance in the 1950's. In 1871, the House of Commons held their sessions here, and from 1876 to 1879, so did the Senate.

DINNER GIVEN BY NAPOLEON III FOR QUEEN VICTORIA AND PRINCE ALBERT IN THE OPERA OF THE CHATEAU OF VERSAILLES, AUGUST 25, 1855

**PRINCESS PALATINE,
VERSAILLES,
DECEMBER 8, 1701**
"Every day I hear:
There will be a new
opera today,
tomorrow a new
comedy. This year
there have been six
new comedies and
three new operas,
nothing like this has
ever happened
before."

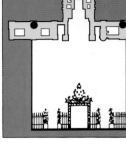

THE MUSEUM OF FRENCH HISTORY

Louis-Philippe, who initiated the idea of the Museum of French History at Versailles, wanted to reconcile all political parties as well as glorify his own government. With this in mind he set about collecting authentic or apocryphal works from all periods of French history. The preface of the first catalog described the project's goal: "To devote the former residence of Louis XIV to all the glories of France, to gather within its walls mementos of our past..." After the fall of Louis-Philippe, the various governments which followed in France continued this policy. Since then, an effort has been made to streamline the collections, and only contemporary paintings or sculptures of the events are exhibited.

COMTE RODOLPHE APPONYI (ATTACHÉ AT THE AUSTRIAN EMBASSY UNDER LOUIS-PHILIPPE), JOURNAL

"It would take far more time and space than I have today to describe the wonders of this restored palace, renovated, younger by a century, a blaze of freshly polished marble, shining with a former luxury that amazed the most sumptuous century of modern times, and which amazes us far more today, when all is small and mediocre compared to a monument such as the château of Versailles [...] All these halls and apartments representing events in France's history. There are portraits of illustrious men of all callings; whether the picture is true or false is of little importance, there are scientists and beauties, warriors and courtiers, Napoleon in all his military glory, Napoleon represented, with his Court, in stage costumes all of white satin embroidered with gold and silver."

LOUIS-PHILIPPE AND HIS SONS LEAVING THE CHATEAU OF VERSAILLES

BY HORACE VERNET

THE CRUSADES ROOM

In order to retrace the history of France from its origins to his reign, Louis-Philippe called upon the most famous historical painters of his time. The Crusades, so dear to the hearts of the Romantics, are presented in a neo-Gothic decor, characteristic of the "troubadour" taste of the Romantic period. The ceilings are embellished with the coats of arms of knights who distinguished themselves during the Crusades, and the furniture is directly inspired by the novels of Sir Walter Scott and Victor Hugo.

CLAUDE BALLIN
GOLDSMITH

THE 17TH CENTURY ROOMS

After crossing the entrance hall, called the Gabriel Vestibule, and the Lower Chapel Vestibule, the tour of the château begins with the rooms on the ground floor and the first floor of the North Wing on the garden side.

The rooms in this part of the château were once the princes' apartments, but were destroyed when Louis-Philippe transformed Versailles into a museum.

These rooms contain 17th century iconography and therefore serve as an introduction to the history of the château, and the tour of its apartments.

After the reigns of Louis XIV's predecessors, the visitor will see depictions of the regency of Anne of Austria, the Fronde and the Jansenist movement, the first artists of Versailles and France's foreign policy at the beginning of Louis XIV's reign.

The young King wished to add to his military and diplomatic successes the prestige of a refined civilization, and was fortunate enough to work with a host of talented artists.

The last rooms on the ground floor conjure up Court life, its receptions, its festivities, the brilliant entourage of the young ruler and, finally, interest in the development of the sciences.

VERSAILLES IN 1668

BY PIERRE PATEL

LOUIS XIV,
PROTECTOR OF
THE SCIENCES
BY TESTELIN

Two rooms on the first floor contain works depicting different episodes from Louis XIV's wars. The views of the Royal Châteaux are a reminder of the King's passion for buildings. These are followed by portraits of painters and sculptors who worked on their decoration. Louis XIV's close entourage, his ministers and the royal family are portrayed in the following rooms where several masterpieces by Mignard are displayed. In the last room before the Upper Chapel Vestibule, a large tapestry cartoon of the audience granted by Louis XIV to the Doge of Genoa at Versailles on May 15, 1685 depicts the King in the Hall of Mirrors, adorned with its silver furniture. Several pieces of furniture, most of which were made according to the technique of the famous cabinet maker André-Charles Boulle, accompany the paintings and pieces of sculpture which decorate over twenty rooms.

HAMADRYADE,
TERRACOTTA
SCULPTURE
ON THE FIRST
FLOOR OF
THE NORTH
WING

HENRI
DE LA TOUR
D'AUVERGNE
VICOMTE
DE TURENNE,
SKETCH BY LE BRUN

GROUND-FLOOR PLAN OF THE CHATEAU

The Dauphine's Apartment
1 First Antechamber
2 Second Antechamber
3 State Cabinet
4 Bedchamber
5 Private Cabinet
6 Private Rooms of the Duchesse
  d'Angoulême

The Dauphin's Apartment
7 Library
8 State Cabinet
9 Bedchamber
10 Private Rooms
11 Second Antechamber
12 Galerie basse (Lower Gallery)

Madame Victoire's Apartment
13 First Antechamber
14 Salon des Nobles
15 State Cabinet
16 Bedchamber
17 Private Cabinet
18 Library

Madame Adélaïde's Apartment
19 Private Cabinet
20 Bedchamber
21 State Cabinet
22 Salle des Hocquetons (Archers' Room) formerly
  the antechambers to the apartment,
  and drawing-room of the Ambassadors' Staircase
23 Vestibule to the Ambassadors' Staircase
24 Vestibule
25 Room of the King's Guard
26 King's Staircase

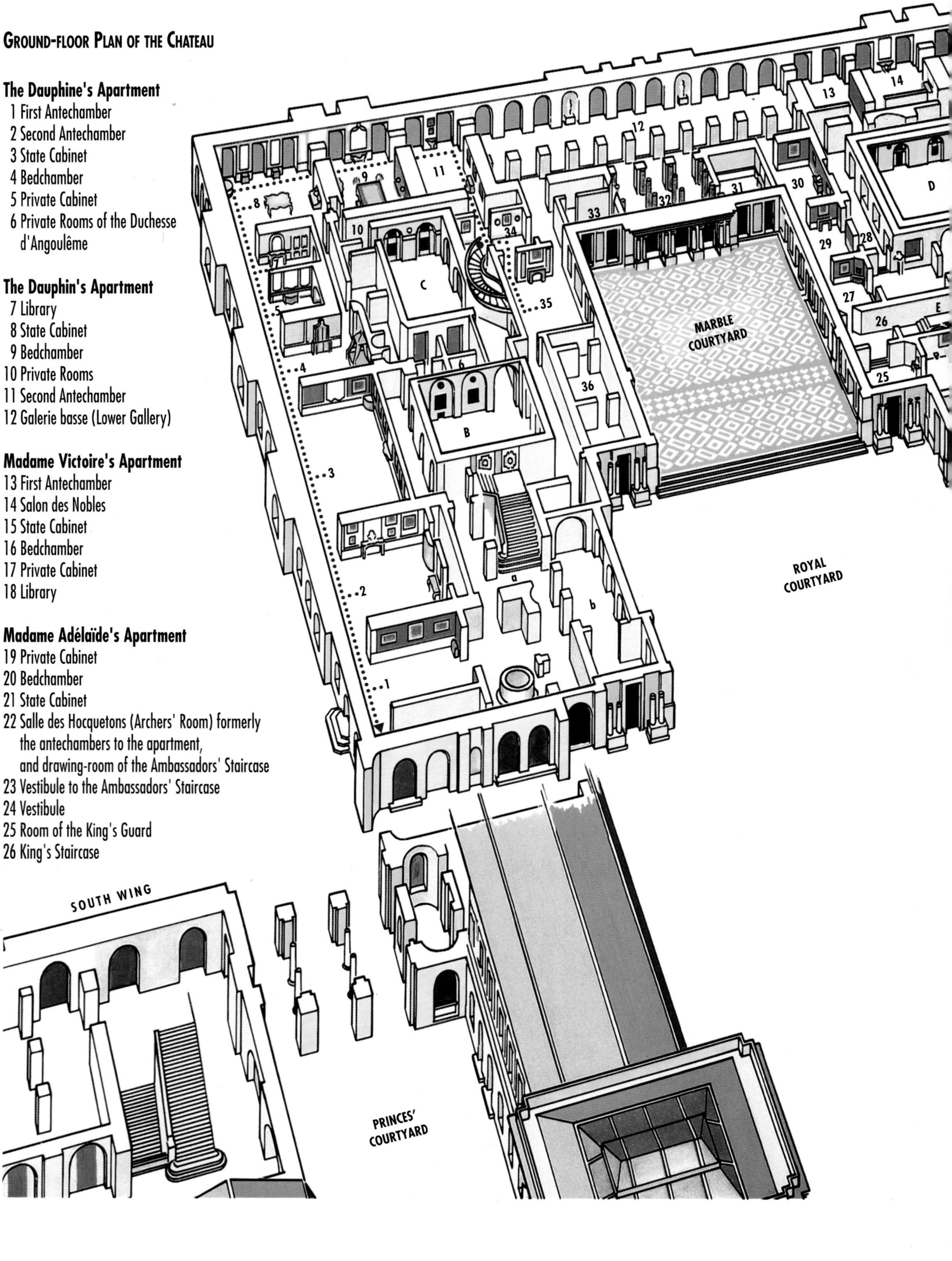

MARBLE COURTYARD

ROYAL COURTYARD

SOUTH WING

PRINCES' COURTYARD

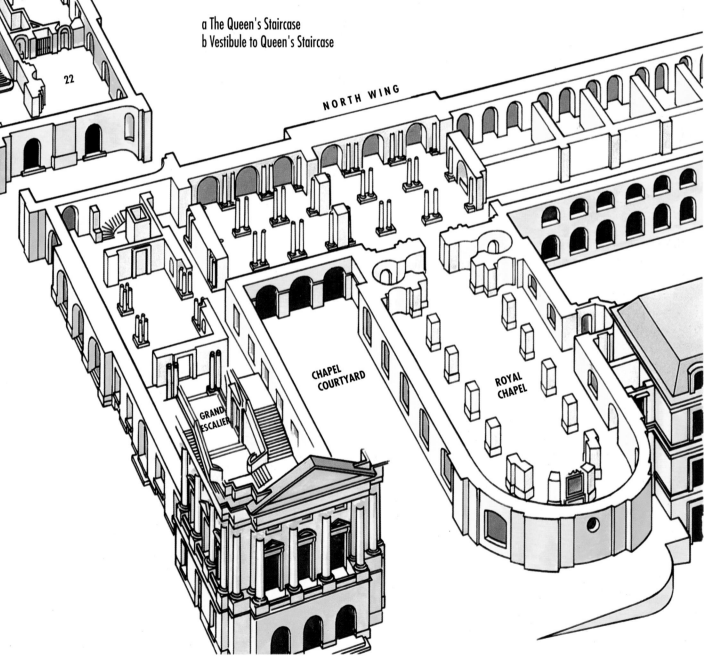

The Captain of the Guard's Apartment
27 State Cabinet
28 Private Cabinet
29 Bedchamber

Marie-Antoinette's Apartment
30 (Room 30)
31 Queen's Bedchamber
32 Central Vestibule
33 Bathroom

Entrance Rooms of the Dauphin's Apartment
34 First Antechamber
35 Guard Room

The King's Wardrobe
36 (rooms 35, 36, 37)

a The Queen's Staircase
b Vestibule to Queen's Staircase

B Monseigneur's or Queen's Courtyard
C Dauphin's or Queen's Courtyard
D Cour des Cerfs (Courtyard of the Stags)
E The King's Staircase
F The King's Private Courtyard

.... Tour of King's Bedchamber

NORTH WING

CHAPEL COURTYARD

GRAND ESCALIER

ROYAL CHAPEL

MARIE-LECZINSKA (1703-1768), BY NATTIER

THE 18TH CENTURY ROOMS

When the Museum of French History was created, the apartments on the ground floor of the palace's central part, which had once belonged to the Dauphins de France, La Dauphine, mother of Louis XVI, Madame de Pompadour and the daughters of Louis XV, were sacrificed.

During the first reorganization of the museum in the early 1900's, paintings depicting the 18th century were displayed here. Today, by means of a certain number of wood panels preserved here or found in the château's reserves, several of the rooms where the Children of France lived under Louis XV and Louis XVI have been recreated. These rooms, overlooking the South Parterre and going as far as the so-called Lower Gallery, include the apartments of the Dauphin, son of Louis XV, and Maria-Josepha of Saxony (with the Prince's Bedchamber, State Cabinet, Library,

THE CENTRAL VESTIBULE OR MARBLE VESTIBULE

the Princess' Private Cabinet), as well as several small rooms decorated under the Restoration for the Duchesse d'Angoulême, Louis XVI's daughter, when Louis XVIII was considering living at Versailles.

After the Lower Gallery, overlooking the North Parterre, are the apartments of Mesdames Adélaïde and Victoire, Louis XV's daughters; these rooms are also being restored. Under Louis XIV, these apartments contained the King's Bathing Apartment.

Several rooms around the Marble Courtyard have been recreated; they include the Guards Room, the apartment of the captain of the guards, as well as part of the small apartments Marie-Antoinette had built after Madame Sophie's death in 1783.

These rooms have a dual nature: they form a part of the Museum of French History, and because of their renovation, they bear witness to the lifestyle prior to the creation of this museum.

THE DAUPHIN'S
BEDCHAMBER

THE DAUPHIN'S
STATE CABINET

MADAME
VICTOIRE'S
STATE CABINET

PRINCESS PALATINE,
MARLY,
FEBRUARY 18, 1712.
"I thought I had
finished telling you
sad news, with the
exception of the
painful ceremony I
attended yesterday
at Versailles; but
disaster has struck
once again. Our
good Crown Prince
has followed his
wife to the grave, he
died at eight thirty.
I'm sure you can
imagine how
disconsolate we all
are here. The king's
pain is so great that
I fear for his health
[…] As the king has
an awful cold, he
was not wakened,
but was given the
terrible news when
he awoke."

THE REVOLUTION ROOMS

Four rooms on the Chimay attic storey are dedicated to the Revolution, the first signs of which took place at Versailles. One of the key works displayed here is the great sketch by David of The Jeu de Paume Oath of Allegiance. The events of 1792 are also represented: Louis XVI as a constitutional monarch by Carteaux, and The Capture of the Tuileries on August 10, 1792 by Berteaux.

During the invasion of the palace by the mob, the unfinished pastel of Marie-Antoinette by Kurcharsky was pierced twice by a pike; these gashes are still visible.

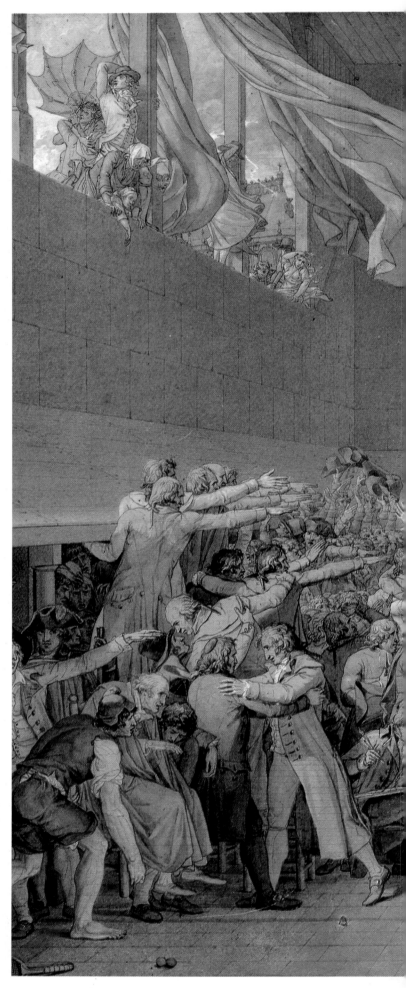

THE CONSULATE AND THE EMPIRE

In Versailles, Louis-Philippe gathered almost all the paintings commissioned by Napoleon I to extol his own glory. This was not due to an inordinate love of the Empire, but the descendent of Louis XIII realized the historical interest of these works kept in the reserves since the second abdication of Napoleon I. By treating the imperial epoch like any other period of French history, he also hoped to neutralize the last remaining supporters of that turbulent era.

The rooms on the ground floor of the South Wing are a memento of the "Citizen-King's" wishes, whereas the more recent arrangement of the attic provides a stricter chronology of the Empire.

NAPOLÉON BEFORE THE TOWN OF AUGSBOURG
BY GAUTHEROT

LOUIS-PHILIPPE
BY WINTERHALTER

CHARLES X
ENTERING PARIS
AFTER HIS
CORONATION
BY LEJEUNE

THE 19TH CENTURY ROOMS

Each of the regimes which followed the 1848 Revolution continued to enrich the collections of the Museum of French History. In the 19th century, the rooms in the North Wing attic, on the garden side, as well as seven large rooms on the first floor of the same building overlooking the rue des Réservoirs and the interior courtyards were set aside for this purpose.

Only the lack of space and the style of contemporary painters prevented the continuation of this vast panorama of French history, begun by a King who yearned for the reconciliation of his subjects.

In addition to the rulers of France and their families, these rooms house 19th century paintings depicting the Colonial conquests, as well as portraits of writers such as Lamartine and Victor Hugo.

GENERAL PLAN OF THE VERSAILLES ESTATE

1 The South Parterre
2 The Orangery
3 The Water Parterre
4 The Latona Fountain and Parterre
5 The North and South Quincunxes
6 The Bosquet des Rocailles
7 The Queen's Grove
8 The Mirror Pond and the King's Garden
9 The Fountain of Autumn
10 The Fountain of Winter
11 The Salle des Marroniers
12 The Colonnade
13 The Royal Avenue or Tapis Vert
14 The Fountain of Apollo and the Grand Canal
15 The Fountain of Enceladus
16 The Bosquet des Dômes
17 The Obelisk
18 The Fountain of Spring
19 The Fountain of Summer
20 The Bosquet de l'Etoile (Star Grove)
21 The Children's Island and the Rond Vert
22 The Baths of Apollo
23 The North Parterre
24 The Pyramid and Bathing Nymphs
25 The Water Avenue
26 The Dragon Fountain
27 The Fountain of Neptune

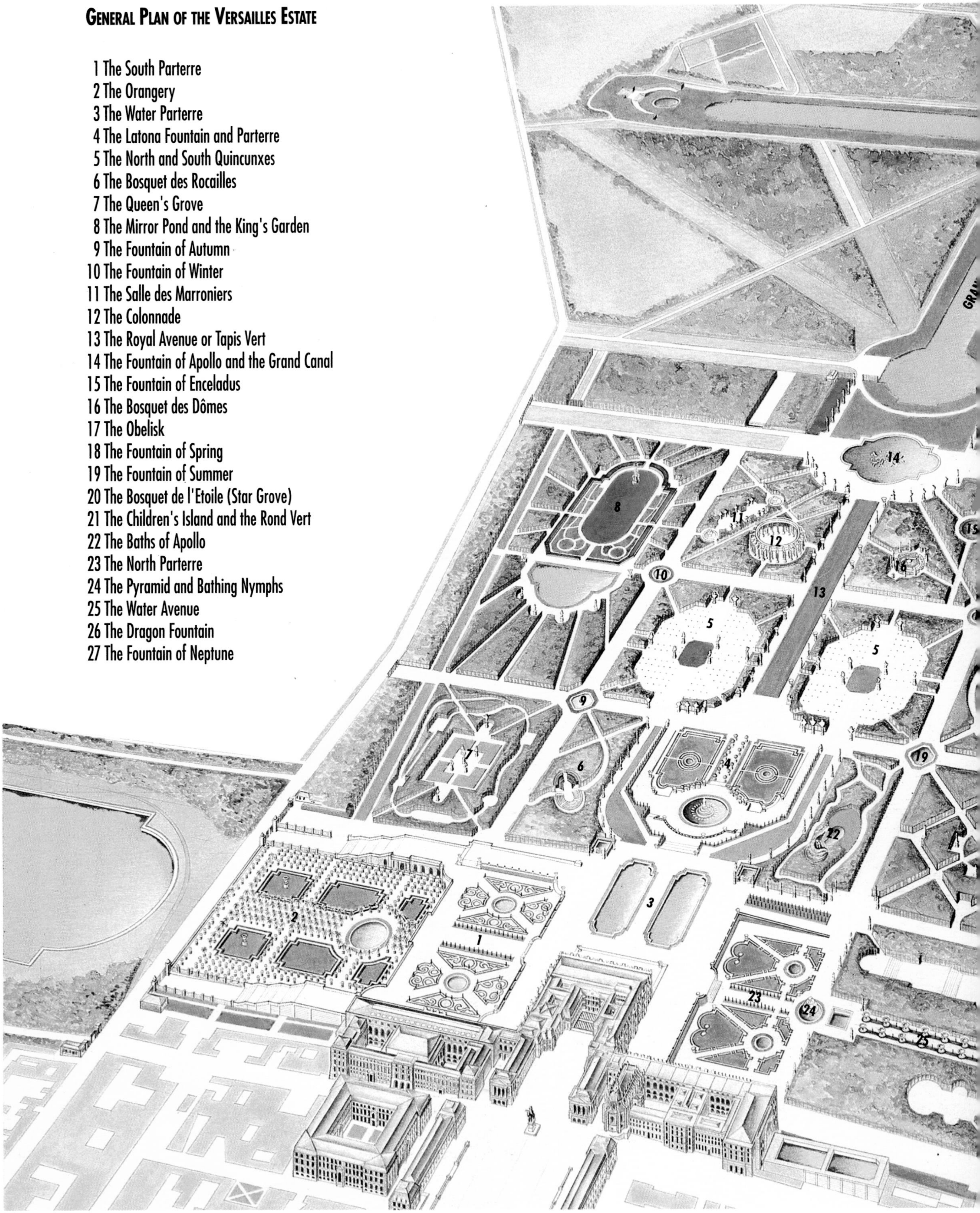

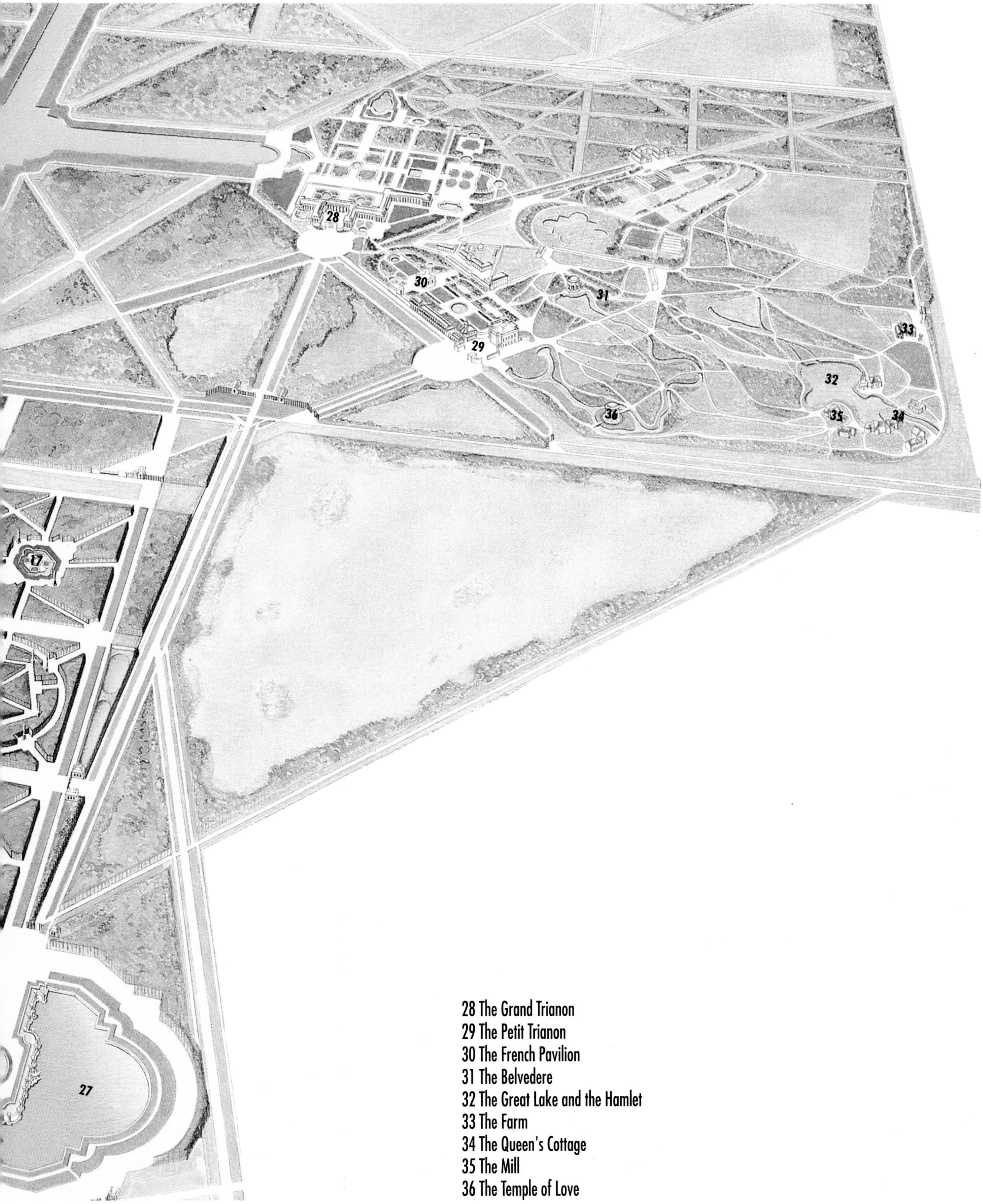

28 The Grand Trianon
29 The Petit Trianon
30 The French Pavilion
31 The Belvedere
32 The Great Lake and the Hamlet
33 The Farm
34 The Queen's Cottage
35 The Mill
36 The Temple of Love

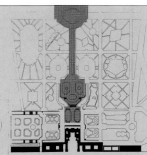

THE GARDENS OF VERSAILLES

THE WATER PARTERRE
THE PARTERRE OF LATONA
THE GREEN CARPET
THE FOUNTAIN OF APOLLO
THE GRAND CANAL

Louis XIV began staying in Versailles as early as 1661. At the time, the park surrounding the small hunting pavilion built by Louis XIII was rather rudimentary. But the Sun King became deeply interested in improving his gardens and called upon André Le Nôtre (1613-1700). By 1664, a great many projects had already been completed in the château as well as in the park, and on May 7-9, the King hosted a spectacular event known as the Pleasures of the Enchanted Island. This event was such a success that the King gave another gala, called the Great Royal Entertainment of Versailles, the night of July 18, 1668. Six years later, to celebrate the second conquest of the Franche-Comté, five days of festivities were organized between July 4 and August 31, 1674. The park already had the general structure which we see today: a main east-west axis, with two secondary axes, running parallel, to the north and south. Perpendicular to the great axes are four north-south avenues which mark out 14 sectors in which Le Nôtre, followed by Jules Hardouin-Mansart (1645-1708), progressively created groves and fountains. The park's multiple modifications continued for close to forty years. One of the key aspects of this park is its fountains. Their number and diversity were highly acclaimed, but led the King to undertake major architectural work to pump water from the Seine and the Eure out to Versailles. The problem of water supply became apparent early on in the creation of the gardens. Louis XIV first called in two Florentine engineers, the Francini brothers, who installed a pump on the banks of the pond at Clagny. The Marly waterworks, built by Arnold Deville and Rennequin Sualem from 1681 to 1684, carried water from the Seine to Versailles via the Louveciennes aqueduct. An attempt was even made to deviate the course of the Eure River, but this project was interrupted by the war of 1688.

THE CHATEAU AND GARDENS OF VERSAILLES

EARLY IN THE REIGN OF LOUIS XVI

ILLUMINATION OF THE PARK OF VERSAILLES DURING THE WEDDING FESTIVITIES FOR THE DAUPHIN, FUTURE LOUIS XVI, AND ARCHDUCHESS MARIE-ANTOINETTE, MAY 19, 1770

The sculpture decorations of the gardens also evolved during this period. The first sculptures were made of gilt lead or simply painted white, but these were progressively replaced by Italian style white marble statues, some copies of antiquity subjects, others works sculpted from the drawings of Head Painter Charles Le Brun (1619-1690). Around 1684 the first cast bronze statues by the Keller brothers were added to the park. In 1704, since Le Nôtre's death four years earlier, Jules Hardouin-Mansart had directed the remaining modifications and Louis XIV could rightly consider Versailles' park as completed. Louis XV made very few changes to his great-grandfather's creation. But the park was entirely re-planted after the accession of Louis XVI in 1774. Some of the groves were completely altered, including the area around the fountain of Apollo, north of the fountain of Latona, and the Labyrinth, which became the Queen's garden. Two paintings by Hubert Robert, on display in the château, bear witness to these drastic changes.

In 1817, Louis XVIII had the Ile Royale pond drained to create an English-style garden, the King's garden, in front of the Mirror Pond.

COLBERT, ORDERS AND REGULATIONS FOR THE BUILDINGS OF VERSAILLES SEPTEMBER 30, 1672. "Lefèvre must read often the memoranda I leave him of all the work to be done, and he must work with care and diligence in executing all the articles. He must divide up all the various types of work and give specific notes to all the workers carrying them out, and see that they execute the tasks with diligence and in the correct

manner, both as regards resistance and cleanliness. By five o'clock in the morning each day, he shall start an inspection of the work; to check the number of workers for each trade, and include it in his journal or notebook, which he shall have in his pocket in order to give me an exact report each time I come here, or when I ask him for it.

He must keep himself informed and take precise notes on all the work Francines (1), master Le Nostre, and master Denis supervise, all work such as masonry, joinery, carpentry, ironwork, etc., all the earthwork, and so on. He shall receive reports from Robelin (2) concerning the digging of the canal; and as it seems that there is not sufficient work to fill his time, he may use him for other things."

1 - François de Francine, Lord of Grand-Maison, the King's ordinary maître d'hôtel, engineer and general supervisor of fountains, grottos, monuments, aqueducts, water works and piping for the houses, castles and palaces of Paris, Saint-Germain, Fontainebleau, Vincennes.
2 - Marc Robelin, Officer of the Grand Canal at Versailles. He also supervised work on the Marly Aqueduct.

THE WATER PARTERRE

The two reflection pools look like a continuation of the magnificent château facade. Often modified, their definitive appearance wasn't achieved until 1685. The harmony of the sculpture decor was inspired and supervised by Le Brun. From 1687 to 1694, the Keller brothers, metal founders, made bronze castings at the Paris Arsenal of the models carved by Le Brun's sculptors (Tubi, Le Hongre, Regnaudin, Coysevox, etc.). Each reflection pool is adorned with four recumbent statues representing the Rivers of France, four nymphs and four groups of children.

The Water Parterre is not complete without the two Fighting Animals fountains, completed in 1687, which flank the stairway leading to the Fountain of Latona. Inseparable, too, are the six allegorical statues, Air (by Hongre), Evening (by Desjardins), Noon and Daybreak (by G. Marsy), Spring (by Magnier) and Water (by Le Gros), which were part of the "Great Commission" of marble statues placed by Colbert in 1674.

THE LATONA PARTERRE

Inspired by the Metamorphosis by Ovid, the Latona parterre illustrates the legend of Latona, the mother of Diana and Apollo, as she implores Jupiter to avenge her against the peasants of Lycia who scorned her; he turned them into frogs.

This parterre consists of three fountains: the Fountain of Latona and the two Lizard Fountains.

The marble statue of Latona and her children are in the center of the first fountain. Sculpted by the Marsy brothers in 1670, it used to stand on a rock surrounded by six frogs half-emerging from the water, while twenty-four others were arranged outside the basin, on the lawn. The goddess then faced the château.

The fountain was modified by Jules Hardouin-Mansart, between 1687 and 1689. It is now composed of three concentric marble bases on top of which the statue of Latona, raised on a stand, now looks toward the Grand Canal.

Each tier contains carvings of frogs, turtles, and men and women with frog's legs or heads, with over 50 water jets.

The Lizard Fountains, made by the Marsy brothers and cast in lead, are placed symmetrically in the center of the two parterres of flowers and lawn; they also illustrate the legend of the metamorphosis of the Lycian peasants.

The Half-Moon, in front of the Green Carpet, is decorated with ten statues, four groups are carved after classical statues and date from Louis XIV's time: Castor and Pollux (by Coysevox), Aria and Poetus (by Lespingola), Greek Peace (by Carlier and Mosnier), Laocoön and his sons (by Tubi).

**THE FOUNTAIN
OF LATONA**

THE GREEN CARPET

Past the Latona parterre, the Green Carpet (or Royal Avenue), 1099 feet long and 210 feet wide, stretches the perspective down to the Grand Canal. Twelve marble statues and twelve vases decorate this long avenue. Most of these were carved during the 17th century by students of the Academy of France in Rome.

Down a gentle slope, the Green Carpet leads to a reflection pool excavated in 1636, under Louis XIII, and finished by Louis XIV. In 1671, it received Tubi's splendid lead ensemble representing Apollo on his chariot drawn by four horses, surrounded by dolphins and tritons.

Beyond this pool lies the Grand Canal, 5118 feet long and 394 feet wide. Near its center, a cross section, 3323 feet long, stretches from the Menagerie to the Grand Trianon. Digging was begun on the canal in 1668, and it was completed in 1679. A great many water festivities were held here, and in winter, when the canal was frozen over, the Court would skate on it or go sleigh-riding.

Around 1669, Louis XIV commissioned rowboats and reduced-scale ships from Marseille and Le Havre to sail on the canal.

In 1674, the Republic of Venice presented the King with two gondolas and four gondoliers who, along with their families, were housed in the "Little Venice" buildings near the top of the Grand Canal.

VÉNUS
BY FRÉMERY

FÉLIBIEN,
ACCOUNT OF THE
PARTY HELD
AT VERSAILLES
ON JULY 18, 1668.
"Most noteworthy in the park of Versailles is the Grand Canal. It is 33 fathoms wide by 900 fathoms long. Three bodies of water mark the ends and the middle. The first is the one closest to the top which separates the gardens from the large park. The second is in the middle of the Grand Canal and it is crossed by another, 40 fathoms wide which leads to the Trianon on one side, and to the Menagerie on the other. And the third part, which is at the end of the Grand Canal, is 200 fathoms long by 100 fathoms wide."

THE GREEN
CARPET

THE FOUNTAIN OF APOLLO, CIRCA 1725-1730

BY J. RIGAUD

COLBERT, ORDERS AND REGULATIONS FOR THE BUILDINGS OF VERSAILLES.
"He shall frequently inspect all the buildings along the canal, and review the number of men he employs, and send me a certificate every month."

LOUIS XIV, INSTRUCTIONS ON HOW TO SHOW THE GARDENS OF VERSAILLES
"Walk down to the Apollo, and pause to contemplate the figures, the vases along the royal avenue, Latona and the château; also go see the canal. If one wishes to see the Menagerie and Trianon on the same day, this should be done before seeing the other fountains."

APOLLO'S CHARIOT

BY TUBI

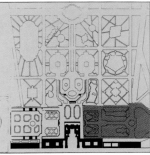

THE NORTH PARTERRE

From the central terrace and the Water Parterre, one goes down several steps to the North Parterre created in 1664. The decor of the château's facades and the fountains is inspired by water divinities. Both sections of the North Parterre are embellished with the Crown Fountains, filled with swimming tritons and sirens, once made of gilded lead, the work of Tubi and Le Hongre.

At the end of the central avenue stands the Pyramid Fountain by Girardon, consisting of four superimposed marble bowls held up by lead sculptures of tritons, dolphins and crayfish. From the Pyramid, an avenue, called the Water Avenue or Avenue of the Marmosets, gently slopes toward the Fountain of Neptune. At the entrance to this avenue is the Fountain of the Bathing Nymphs, a masterpiece by Girardon (1668-1670). The rectangular basin with its cascading water, is decorated with a lead bas-relief of nymphs romping at the water's edge.

COLBERT, REGULATIONS FOR THE FOUNTAINS OF VERSAILLES

"Head fountain master Denis shall always have three journeymen plumbers and six workmen, as stipulated in his contract. All shall be housed in the pump building, according to a distribution to be defined. None of the journeymen or workmen shall reside elsewhere, under pain of being dismissed from employment. None shall be dismissed without notifying us. Master Denis shall assign each a given job, with instruction in the tasks each must execute when the King orders that the fountains function. He shall provide them with keys for the cocks and fittings, and with ladders, whalebone rods, and all other tools necessary to repair the defects of the fountains. Should a journeyman or workman not be on his job when an order is given to that effect, Denis shall be fined one ecu for each journeyman and 30 sols for each workman, unless he makes the same deduction. Should any of them be missing one of the above-mentioned tools in the presence of the King, the same deduction shall be made."

THE NORTH PARTERRE

THE WATER AVENUE

The Water Avenue is lined with twenty-two groups of bronze sculptures of children holding up a bowl of Languedoc marble. These were executed by various 17th century sculptors. On each side of this avenue used to stand two groves: "The Three Fountains" and "Triumphant France".

The King's State Apartment, on the first floor of the château, looks onto this part of the garden. The ground floor on this side used to house his Bathing Apartment, transformed in the 18th century. The Thetis grotto, located on the site of the Lower Chapel Vestibule, was demolished in 1684 to make way for the North Wing.

LOUIS XIV,
INSTRUCTIONS ON
HOW TO SHOW THE
GARDENS OF
VERSAILLES
"Next is the Pyramid; stop a moment, and then climb up to the château using the marble stairs between the Esguiseur and the Shameful Venus, turn at the top of the stairs to see the North Parterre, the statues, the vases, the wreaths, the Pyramid and what can be seen of Neptune, then leave the garden using the same door used to enter it."

COLBERT,
ORDERS AND
REGULATIONS FOR
THE BUILDINGS OF
VERSAILLES
"For all the inspections he makes, he shall continually incite the gardeners to keep all the paths clean, along with the rest."

THE FOUNTAIN OF NEPTUNE

The Fountain of Neptune was built from 1679 to 1681 under the supervision of Le Nôtre. It was slightly modified by Jacques-Ange Gabriel in 1736, and its carved decor was added in 1740. L.-S. Adam created the central group representing Neptune and Amphitrite, Bouchardon the Proteus and the Unicorn group, and J.-B. Lemoyne the god Oceanus. The new fountain was inaugurated by Louis XV and aroused great admiration because of the number, range and variety of the fountains playing on the once-gilded lead sculptures.

THE DRAGON FOUNTAIN

The Water Avenue leads to the semi-circular Dragon Fountain depicting one of the episodes in the story of Apollo: the serpent Python (slain by Apollo) is surrounded by dolphins and cupids with bows and arrows, astride swans. The main water jet reaches a height of 88 feet.
The present sculptures are copies

THE DRAGON
FOUNTAIN
BY THE MARSY BROTHERS

made in 1889 to replace the completely deteriorated 17th century originals carved by the Marsy brothers.

THE FOUNTAIN
OF NEPTUNE

THE SOUTH PARTERRE

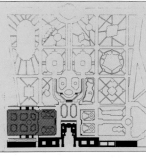

THE ORANGERY

The Queen's Apartment, located on the first floor, looks onto the South Parterre, also known as the "Floral Parterre" or the "Parterre of Love". It is situated above the Orangery built by Jules Hardouin-Mansart.

The South Parterre is reached by a staircase flanked by two of the oldest pieces of sculpture in the park: Children with Sphinxes. The bronze Cupids were modeled by Sarazin, cast by Duval in 1668 and placed on marble sphinxes carved by Lerambert.

At the northern extremity of the balustrade separating the parterre from the groves, stands the fine replica of a classical statue by Van Clève, that of Ariadne Sleeping.

LOUIS XIV, INSTRUCTIONS ON HOW TO SHOW THE GARDENS OF VERSAILLES "Then turn left and pass between the Sphinxes; along the way pause in front of the Cabinet to contemplate the spray and reflection of the water; at the level of the Sphinxes, pause to look at the south parterre, then go straight to the top of the Orangery where one can see the orange tree parterre and the lake of the Swiss Guards."

LOUIS XIV, MEMOIRS FOR THE INSTRUCTION OF A CROWN PRINCE. "I shall not tell you only how a normal individual is told of the reasons why nature has provided us with honest pleasures. I shall not tell you only that they refresh you after work, give you new strength to continue work, soothe the soul, calm troubling passions, inspire humanity, soften manners, and remove any sour quench from virtue, which makes it less sociable and hence less useful. Since, for a Prince and a King of France, these public entertainments, which are not so much ours, as those of our court of our subjects, should be considered as something more. "

THE SOUTH PARTERRE

THE ORANGERY

The Orangery consists of a central arched gallery, 504 feet long, which is extended by two lateral galleries beneath the Stairways of the Hundred Steps. Light enters the whole building through large arched windows. It was built by Jules Hardouin-Mansart from 1684 to 1686, to replace the small orangery erected by Le Vau in 1663.

In front of the main gallery lies the parterre with a round reflection pool and six lawn sections. During the warm seasons, the orange trees, palm trees and oleanders are set outside. The Lake of the Swiss Guards extends the Orangery parterre beyond the Saint-Cyr road. It was dug in 1678, measures 2237 feet by 768 feet, and is flanked by the two Mail avenues. Lying to the east of the lake is the King's vegetable garden, organized by La Quintynie as of 1677.

THE LAKE OF THE SWISS GUARDS AND THE ORANGERY
BY JEAN COTELLE

THE ORANGERY
PARTERRE

LA FONTAINE, LES AMOURS DE PSYCHÉ ET DE CUPIDON
"As our people still had leisure time, they strolled around the Orangery. There are no words to describe the beauty and number of orange trees and other plants there. Some of these trees have withstood the rigors of a hundred winters: Seeing no one but his three friends nearby; Acante could not help but recite a few verses of poetry that the others remembered having seen in a work of his own composition.

Oranges, trees that I adore, How sweet are your perfumes! Is there anything in Flore's empire As pleasant as you?

Your fruits, with their robust shell Are true treasure; The garden of the Hesperides' Apples of gold were none other than they.

Your fruits, with their robust shell Are true treasure; The garden of the Hesperides' Apples of gold were none other than they.

Your flowers perfume all the air I breathe: A gentle zephyr Ever plays around you. You are dwarves; but no giant tree, Waging war on the Sun, Can equal you, though it shade acres of ground "

LOUIS XIV, INSTRUCTIONS ON HOW TO SHOW THE GARDENS OF VERSAILLES
"Descend the right hand stairs of the Orangery, and enter the orange tree garden, go straight to the fountain and from there contemplate the Orangery, walk among the rows of orange trees, then visit the covered Orangery, and exit by the vestibule on the Labyrinth side. "

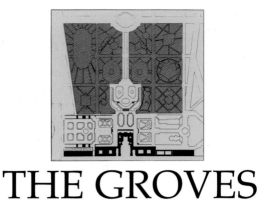

THE GROVES

Under the reign of Louis XIV, the Versailles gardens included 15 groves; these individual gardens enclosed by gates, and with a different layout and decor, were spread throughout the park. Most of them were created by Le Nôtre, such as the Rockwork grove or that of the Domes. When the master gardener died, Jules Hardouin-Mansart modified the decor of a few groves: the Banquet hall or the Council hall became the Obelisk grove, and the Antiquity hall, once replanted, was called the Hall of Chestnut trees. These charming halls of greenery, fantasy havens in such a regular garden, surprised the visitor with various fountains and abundant sculptures. During galas, guests gathered within them for light supers, dancing, music, or just to stroll around. As they were hard to maintain and very expensive, some deteriorated and were closed to the public as early as the 18th century. When the park was completely replanted in 1775-1776, Louis XVI and Marie-Antoinette had the maze changed into the Queen's Grove, and Hubert Robert was asked to transform the Baths of Apollo into the then popular Anglo-Chinese garden style. Under Louis XVIII, the Royal Island was drained and replaced with the King's Garden, filled with exotic and rare trees.

COLBERT, ORDERS AND REGULATIONS FOR THE BUILDINGS OF VERSAILLES. "In the gardens: as soon as possible have Berthier, the rock mason, set up two or three workshops to restore all the rock work; the first, at the grotto, the second, near the Marsh, and the third, at the Theater.

THE ROCKWORK GROVE

Bring in the smelter, and have him carefully inspect all faucets, valves, fittings and all other copper works, to renovate everything. [...] Remove all pine trees along the pyramid alley and that of the waterfall, and plant spruce firs instead "

138

THE ROCKWORK GROVE

This grove, created by Le Nôtre between 1680 to 1683, used to be called the Ballroom "because of a sort of arena on which one dances when it pleases his Majesty to hold a celebration." This "arena" disappeared at the beginning of the 18th century, but the rising tiers and rockwork for which the grove became famous can still be seen. Water streams down in a cascade on the rockwork, made of Madagascar shells. Banks support the tiers where the spectators used to sit during the festivities; the orchestra would sit at the top. Four gilt lead vases by Le Hongre and four candelabra by Mazeline and Jouvenet add to the decor of this grove, one of the few, in the gardens of Versailles, to have retained its original appearance.

THE QUEEN'S GROVE

The Queen's Grove, as we see it today, was created in 1775-1776, when the park was replanted by order of Louis XVI. It is an English-style garden and replaced the famous Maze of Versailles, built in 1666 from plans by Le Nôtre. Each bend in the many little alleys revealed one of 39 fountains.

The subject of each of them had been taken from Aesop's fables and summed up in a quatrain by Benserade engraved in the stand. The lead animals were painted in white.

At the entrance of the Maze, two statues of Aesop and Cupid welcomed visitors. These works, of a rare naturalistic quality, were carved by the best sculptors of Louis XIV's time: Le Hongre, Mazeline, Houzeau, Tubi, etc.

This lovely area, so highly praised in every 17th century guidebook, unfortunately deteriorated to such an extent that it disappeared in 1774. However, a few of these sculptures still exist and are kept in the château of Versailles.

THE QUEEN'S GROVE

THE QUINCUNXES

Through the curtain of trees one glimpses the Quincunxes which have replaced groves now gone: to the north, the Grove of the Dauphin, and, to the south, the Chandelier Grove.

Each Quincunx is decorated by terms commissioned by the Superintendent, Fouquet, for his château at Vaux-le-Vicomte and carved in Rome after models by Poussin. This set of terms, representing the seasons and gods of mythology, was completed by Théodon with his carvings of a "Harvester" and "Winter."

VIEW OF THE QUINCUNXES

THE MIRROR POOL AND THE KING'S GARDEN

The Mirror Pool used to be situated at one end of a pond called the Island of Love or Royal Island (1674), where reduced models of the royal flotilla's war ships were tested. Located in a swampy part of the park and neglected during the Revolution, the Royal Island was drained in 1817 by order of Louis XVIII. This was the work of the architect Dufour, who replaced it with the King's Garden. This closed, English-style garden is carefully planted with exotic and rare trees. The Mirror Pool (or Vertugadin), separated from the Royal Island by an avenue, is all that remains of the original layout.

THE KING'S GARDEN

THE FOUNTAIN OF BACCHUS

The octagonal-shaped Fountain of Bacchus or Autumn was created by the Marsy brothers (1672-1674). The god is represented crowned with vine branches and surrounded by little satyrs reclining on an abundant harvest, its bunches of grapes dipping into the water.

"This is the island of Autumn … the god of wine lies on the golden harvest. What secret has his drunkenness revealed to him that he should smile so mysteriously… His figure has the robustness of a young animal's body and the grace of feminine beauty. He throws handfuls of grapes into the urn while, around him, goat-footed children drink from vessels or press the vermilion fruit between their lips. Here, a satiated little satyr has fallen asleep, there another attempts to make a goat swallow the contents of a ewer." Pierre de Nolhac

BACCHUS

BY THE MARSY BROTHER'S

THE FOUNTAIN OF SATURN

In ancient Rome, the celebrations of Saturn, a god of mythology, took place in December as he represented Winter and the passing of time. This fountain is the work of Girardon (1672-1677).
"He has the great outspread wings of Time and the deep wrinkles of the years … on his lips the bitter expression of the gods who must live forever and would prefer to die." Pierre de Nolhac

COLBERT, ORDERS AND REGULATIONS FOR THE BUILDINGS OF VERSAILLES
"The Fountain of Saturn: the final model shall be executed, and worked on all winter […] Remove the bad soil from the path between Saturn and Apollo; dig trenches and fill them with good soil to plant box-wood bushes. Replant maples anywhere they may be lacking along the sidewalk."

THE FOUNTAIN OF SATURN

THE HALL OF CHESTNUT TREES

Through this oval grove, formerly called the Hall of Classical Statues or Water Gallery and organized from 1680 to 1683, once ran a central pathway lined with orange trees, pruned yews, reflection pools and fountains. Twenty-four classical statues once stood on the periphery of this pathway. Entirely rearranged in 1704, this grove became the Hall of Chestnut trees in the 18th century. It was adorned with eight classical busts and two statues. All that remains of the grove's original decor is its current shape and two small pools at both ends.

THE HALL OF
CHESTNUT TREES

THE COLONNA-
DE GROVE,
CIRCA 1725-
1730 (DÉTAIL)
BY J. RIGAUD

THE COLONNADE

Construction of the Colonnade began in 1685. Its striking architectural design is the work of Jules Hardouin-Mansart, who replaced a grove created by Le Nôtre in 1679: the Grove of the Springs.

This perfectly circular peristyle measures 106 feet in diameter; 32 Ionic columns made of violet brecciated, Languedoc and slate-blue marble, coupled with 32 Languedoc marble pilasters, support the arches and a white marble cornice topped by 32 urns. The triangular tympana between the arches are decorated with bas-reliefs, mostly cupids playing music, thus evoking the original purpose of this grove, that of a concert site. The keystones of the arches are decorated with heads of nymphs, naiads, etc. These are the work of Coysevox, Tubi, Le Hongre, Le Conte, Mazière, Van Clève, etc.

In the center of the Colonnade, a circular marble base holds the famous sculpture made by Girardon (1678-1699): *The Rape of Persephone by Pluto*. The original statue, greatly affected by pollution, has been replaced with a molding.

LOUIS XIV,
INSTRUCTIONS ON
HOW TO SHOW THE
GARDENS OF
VERSAILLES
"Enter the colonnade, go to the center, and walk around it to contemplate the columns, cornice, bas-reliefs and pools. When exiting, stop to see the Guidy sculpture and walk toward the royal avenue."

THE COLONNADE
GROVE

THE GROVE OF THE DOMES

When Le Nôtre first created this grove in 1675, the center of the pool contained a lead figure of Fame, sending forth a powerful jet of water from her trumpet. The octagonal reflection pool was surrounded by a base wall adorned with 44 bas-reliefs, each representing all the weapons used by the different nations of the world. In 1677, Hardouin-Mansart built two white marble domed pavilions standing opposite each other. They were decorated with trophies and gilt bronze bas-reliefs. After falling into disrepair, the Dome pavilions were finally demolished in 1820.

During the reign of Louis-Philippe, the statues installed in 1704 around the grove were sent to Saint-Cloud and not returned to Versailles until 1872. The statues include *Galatea*, by Tubi, *Aurora* by Magnier, *Acis* by Tubi, *Daybreak* by Le Gros, *Ino* by Rayol, a nymph by Flamen, and *Arion* by Raon.

LOUIS XIV, INSTRUCTIONS ON HOW TO SHOW THE GARDENS OF VERSAILLES "PASS BY THE ENCELADUS, WALK ONLY HALF-WAY AROUND THE POOL, AND AFTER CONTEMPLATING IT, EXIT BY THE LOWER PART."

THE FOUNTAIN OF ENCELADUS

The Fountain of Enceladus was cast in lead by Gaspard Marsy, from 1675 to 1677, and was formerly gilded. The subject is taken from the story of the fall of the Titans, who were crushed under the rocks of Mount Olympus after they had tried to scale it despite Jupiter's threats. The sculptor has represented the giant half crushed beneath the rocks, fighting against death. The grove created by Le Nôtre has deteriorated over the centuries, and is currently being restored to its original appearance.

THE FOUNTAIN OF ENCELADUS, BY LE PAUTRE

THE FOUNTAIN OF ENCELADUS

THE OBELISK
GROVE, CIRCA
1725-1730
BY J. RIGAUD

THE OBELISK
THE FOUNTAIN
OF SPRING
THE FOUNTAIN
OF SUMMER

CERES

The Obelisk Fountain was built by Jules Hardouin-Mansart in 1704, on the site of the former Banquet Hall or Council Chamber, created by Le Nôtre in 1671. The lead decorations were then used to adorn the fountains in the Grand Trianon's gardens.

The Fountain of Flora or Spring is round and was carved by Tubi (1672-1677). The goddess, half-naked, reclines on a bed of flowers, surrounded by young cupids playing at weaving garlands.

The contemporary group in the Fountain of Ceres or Summer is the work of Regaudin. It shows the goddess holding a sickle, and around her on the ground, covered with cut wheat, lie naked cupids.

CHILDREN'S ISLAND

To the north of the gardens, between the Star Grove and the Green Ring, and far from the busy avenues, a circular pool with a rock in the center is concealed from view. This is the Children's Island, a masterpiece of spontaneity by Hardy (1710). On the rock, six naked children play with flowers while two others splash about in the water. The charming grace of their poses will not fail to delight the wanderer who discovers this isolated grove.

COLBERT, ORDERS AND REGULATIONS FOR THE BUILDINGS OF VERSAILLES "He must remove all works that are too weak, and be especially careful that none of the faucets, valves and fittings leak, and make sure that all the holes for the faucets are the same size. [...] Inspect every pump twice a week. Make sure that nothing is missing and always have a second set of shafts, boards and bolts for all the devices, and more generally, everything that may cause them to break down."

FOUNTAIN OF THE CHILDREN'S ISLAND

CAST LEAD FIGURES BY HARDY

THE BATHS OF APOLLO

THE BATHS OF APOLLO

The Grove of Apollo's Baths, as we see it nowadays, date from 1776, when the park of Versailles was entirely replanted. It replaced a famous grove, called the "Marsh", which had been created during the reign of Louis XIV, between 1670 and 1673, under the influence of Madame de Montespan.

On this site in 1704, Jules Hardouin-Mansart prepared a new grove to receive the Sun Horses, which had been in the Grove of the Domes since the destruction of the Thetis grotto. This ensemble, carved between 1664 and 1672, is composed of three groups: Apollo being tended by the Nymphs, with four main statues by Girardon and the other three, farther back, by Regnaudin; the two groups of Sun Horses by Guérin and the Marsy brothers. The three groups were sheltered under gilt lead canopies, atop a base wall placed in a pool.

This situation lasted until 1776. At that time, one year after Louis XVI's order to replant the park, the painter Hubert Robert was asked to design a project for the new Baths of Apollo. The project he created and finished in 1778 adopted the popular style of the Anglo-Chinese garden. A huge artificial rock adorned with columns is supposed to represent the palace of Thetis; it houses the three famous groups of sculptures.

GENERAL PLAN OF TRIANON

1 - The Gate of Honour
2 - The Courtyard of Honour
3 - The Gallery
4 - The Trianon-in-the-Woods-Wing
5 - The Upper Garden
6 - The lower Garden
7 - The Horseshoe Fountain
8 - The Mirror Basin
9 - The Knifegrinder (marble)
10 - The Round Fountain
11 - The Water Buffet or Cascade
12 - Circular pool
13 - The Green Hall
14 - Circular pool
15 - Square pool
16 - Parterre
17 - The Hall of Classical Statues
18 - Pool with "ears"
19 - Centaur with tied hands
20 - Former "Garden of the Springs"
21 - Tiered Fountain
22 - The King's Garden
23 - Circular Pool
24 - The French Pavilion
25 - Octagonal pool
26 - The Trellis Pavilion
27 - Octagonal pool
28 - Buildings on site of
     "New Menagerie" and
     "Icecellars"
29 - The Gardener's Cottage
30 - Marie-Antoinette's
     Theatre
31 - The French Garden
32 - Circular pool
33 - The Small Trianon
34 - The Trianon
     Courtyard
35 - The Garden
36 - The Belvedere
37 - The Grotto
38 - The Orangery
39 - The Temple of Love
40 - The Farm
41 - The Great Lake
42 - The Processing Dairy
43 - The Marlborough Tower
     and the Fishery
44 - The site of the Barn
45 - The Preparation Dairy
46 - The Caretaker's House
47 - the Dovecot
48 - The Queen's Cottage
49 - The Billiard Room
50 - The "Rechauffoir"
51 - The Boudoir
52 - The Mill

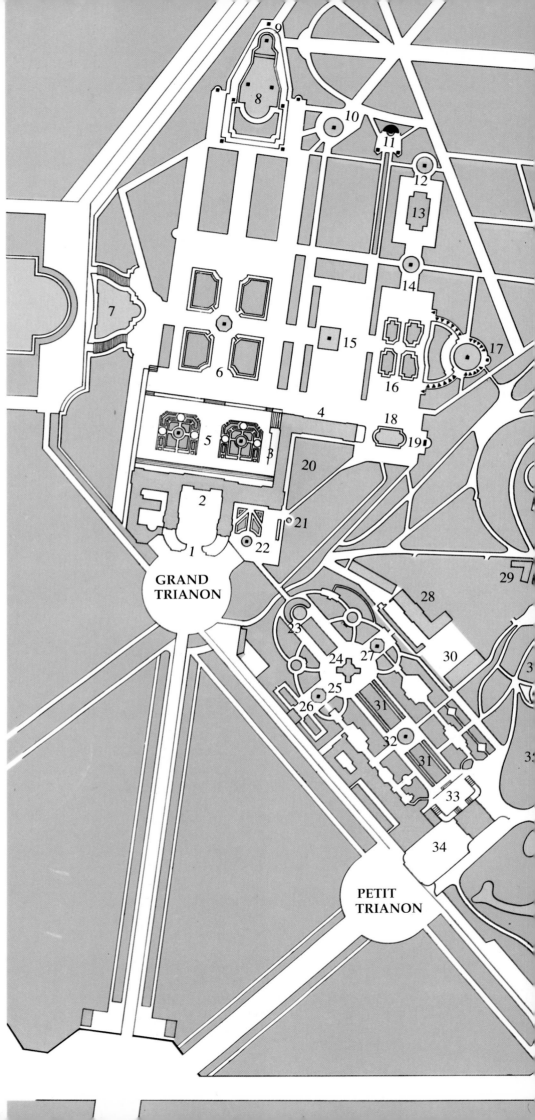

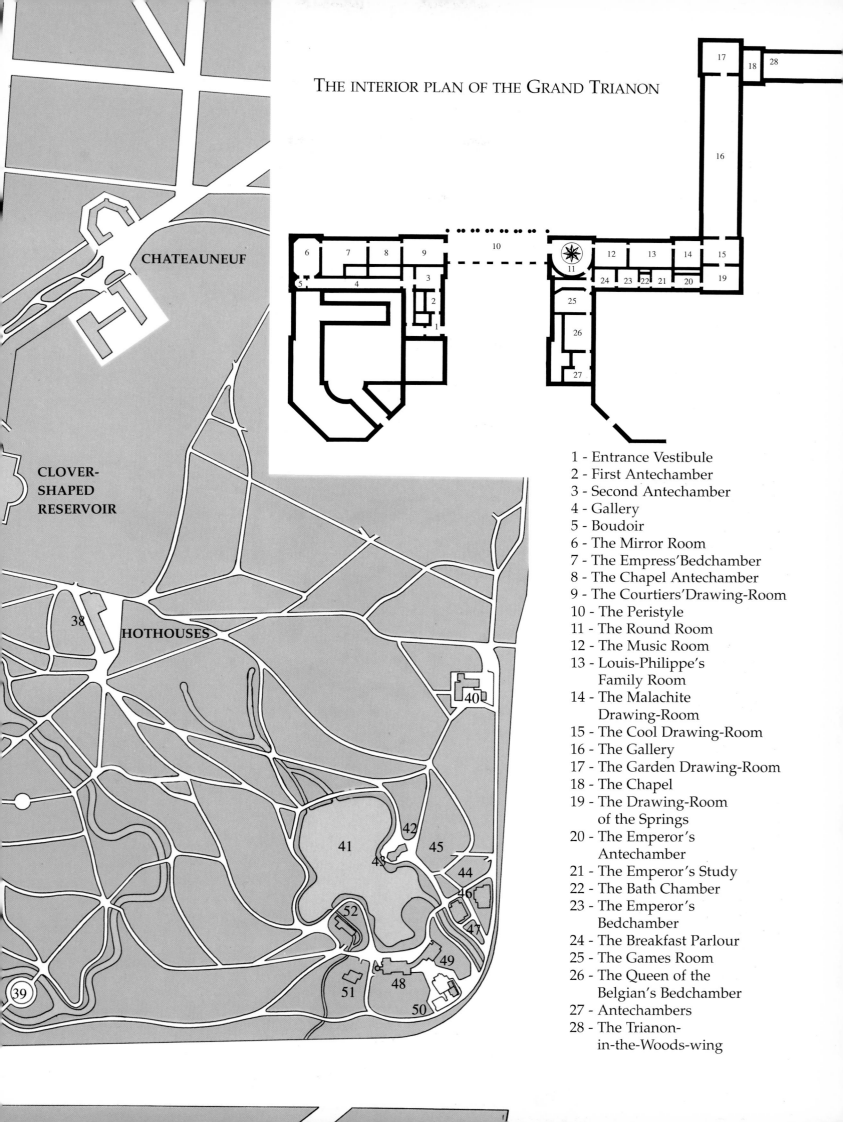

THE INTERIOR PLAN OF THE GRAND TRIANON

CHATEAUNEUF

CLOVER-
SHAPED
RESERVOIR

HOTHOUSES

1 - Entrance Vestibule
2 - First Antechamber
3 - Second Antechamber
4 - Gallery
5 - Boudoir
6 - The Mirror Room
7 - The Empress' Bedchamber
8 - The Chapel Antechamber
9 - The Courtiers' Drawing-Room
10 - The Peristyle
11 - The Round Room
12 - The Music Room
13 - Louis-Philippe's
   Family Room
14 - The Malachite
   Drawing-Room
15 - The Cool Drawing-Room
16 - The Gallery
17 - The Garden Drawing-Room
18 - The Chapel
19 - The Drawing-Room
   of the Springs
20 - The Emperor's
   Antechamber
21 - The Emperor's Study
22 - The Bath Chamber
23 - The Emperor's
   Bedchamber
24 - The Breakfast Parlour
25 - The Games Room
26 - The Queen of the
   Belgian's Bedchamber
27 - Antechambers
28 - The Trianon-
   in-the-Woods-wing

TRIANON

The building of stone and marble we see here today is not the first château built at Trianon. In 1670, on the site of a village bought by Louis XIV in 1668, the architect Le Vau built the Porcelain Trianon, so called because its exterior was decorated with blue and white faience tiles. This first Trianon was a fragile building used for taking light refreshments. By 1687, it was on the verge of falling into ruin; moreover, its small size and style no longer suited the King.

Jules Hardouin-Mansart was commissioned to build the Marble Trianon now present. The idea of the peristyle linking the two wings running into the gardens came from Robert de Cotte. A gallery was added at right angles to the end of the Right Wing, and perpendicular to that, the so-called Trianon-in-the-Woods wing. The doors and windows overlooking both the courtyard and gardens are separated by pink Languedoc marble pilasters. Louis XV had Jussieu and Richard create a botanical garden to the east of the Grand Trianon. In 1750, he asked Gabriel to construct a small pavilion (the French Pavilion) and, from 1749 to 1753, a menagerie. Soon afterwards, the sovereign decided he wanted a smaller château, and the result was the Petit Trianon, built from 1762 to 1768.

THE GRAND TRIANON, CIRCA 1724
BY P.-D. MARTIN

SAINT-SIMON, MEMOIRS.
"The porcelain Petit Trianon, built for Mme de Montespan, bored the King, who wanted palaces everywhere. He took great pleasure in his buildings.

He also had an eye for precision, proportion, symmetry; but taste did not respond, as will be seen later. This palace was barely started when the King perceived a defect in one of the newly-completed casements on the ground floor. Louvois, who was very quick-tempered, and so

spoiled as to find it hard to accept being corrected by his master, argued long and hard, and insisted there was nothing wrong with the casement. The King turned away and walked off to another part of the building. The next day he sought out Le Nostre, a good architect, yet known for gardens, which he was the first to introduce in France and which he cultivated to perfection. The King asked him if he had been to Trianon; he replied he had not. The King explained what had shocked him, and asked that he go there. The next day, the same question, the same answer; and again the following day. The King saw Le Nostre didn't dare say he was wrong, or blame Louvois. He lost his temper, and ordered him to be at Trianon the next day when he would be there and where he would also find Louvois. There was no way out of the dilemma. The King met them both at Trianon the next day. First the window was discussed. Louvois argued; Le Nostre said nothing. Finally the King ordered him to align and measure, then say what he had found. As he worked, Louvois, furious over the verification, fulminated aloud and stated bitterly that the window was exactly the same as the others. The King said nothing and waited; but he was uncomfortable. When all had been examined, he asked Le Nostre what he had found, and Le Nostre stammered. The King exploded, and commanded him to speak clearly. Then Le Nostre admitted the King was right, and said what he found wrong."

THE GRAND TRIANON THE LEFT WING

From 1687 to 1691, the Left Wing of the Grand Trianon held the chapel, its antechamber and the buffet rooms for preparing and serving light refreshments.

In 1691, Louis XIV had an apartment built here which he gave to his son, the grand Dauphin, called Monseigneur, in 1703. The apartment kept the prince's name throughout the 18th century. It was redecorated only after the Revolution: first for Madame Mère, Napoleon's mother, in 1805, and then for Empress Marie-Louise. Under Louis-Philippe, the apartment, with additional rooms built at right angles to it after the Mirror Drawing room, was used by the King and Queen Marie-Amélie.

THE PERISTYLE OF THE GRAND TRIANON

THE MAIN GATEWAY

MARQUIS D'ARGENSON, MAY 16, 1750. "The King enjoys Trianon more than any other house he has resided in as yet: he is starting to tire of his frequent travels, and perhaps he feels a secret desire to limit the expenses of the court, to undertake noble savings in all things; if this were the case, he would be a great king. He says his apartment at Trianon, as it is now arranged, is the only one that is to his liking. It has direct access to the apartment of the marchioness, whom he can see there whenever he wishes; from Trianon, he goes to Versailles on the days and at the times of ceremonies, on Sundays, to concerts, to council meetings if he so wishes: his ministers come to him to work, affairs are carried out there, a play will be held there and I think all this is for the best."

For the sake of convenience, the Left Wing is visited in reverse chronological order. The Mirror Drawing room may thus be admired first, with its decor of mirrors dating from the time of Louis XIV. Because of its particularly pleasant location, this drawing room has always been one of the most important rooms in the apartment. Empress Marie-Louise used it as her State Cabinet, and the various small tables, a pianoforte and even an easel on display were commissioned for her.

The State Bedchamber which follows regained its 17th century proportions about forty years ago. Under the Empire, a partition had been erected to separate the chamber itself from its antechamber. Most of the furniture, however, was here at the time of the 19th century queens and empresses. Of particular note is the bed, which was previously used by Napoleon in the Tuileries, and by Louis XVIII, who died in it in 1824.

THE MIRROR DRAWING ROOM

FÉLIBIEN, ACCOUNT OF THE PARTY HELD AT VERSAILLES ON JULY 18, 1668. "Throughout the château and in the park of Versailles, there are places where each season of the year seems to have its special residence; it is safe to say that Spring always resides at the Trianon. Nothing is more pleasant than the structure of the château, nothing more delicate than its exquisite decorations. It seems to be the home of the Graces and Cupids. The parterres and gardens are always green. Wherever one looks beauty answers back and the air is filled with the perfume of the most fragrant flowers."

THE EMPRESS BEDCHAMBER

THE COURTIERS' DRAWING ROOM

The chapel antechamber draws its name from its original incarnation under Louis XIV. The paintings of the Evangelists, and the cornice with its carvings of grapes and stalks of wheat (symbols of the King's taking communion of bread and wine at his coronation) are a reminder of this event, while the chairs call to mind its use as the main drawing room of Marie-Louise and Marie-Amélie after her. It is preceded by an antechamber, called the Courtiers' Antechamber in the 17th century, which brings the visitor up to the peristyle.

COLBERT, ORDERS AND REGULATIONS FOR THE BUILDINGS OF VERSAILLES. "Visit Trianon often; see that Le Bouteux has flowers for the King throughout the winter, that the right number of workmen are there, and urge him to carry out all the winter work. You must report to me weekly on what flowers were there."

THE PERISTYLE

THE RIGHT WING OF THE GRAND TRIANON

The Right Wing comprises two parallel suites of rooms, one opening onto the upper parterre, the other on to the King's garden. Between 1691 and 1698, the former contained Louis XIV's apartment, which became that of the Duchesse de Bourgogne, Louis XV's mother, who died in 1712. After that date it became the reception suite.

The rooms on the King's garden side underwent many changes in the course of time: first they formed Madame de Maintenon's apartment, then that of Louis XV and Madame de Pompadour. Reserved for sovereigns under Louis XVI, the suite was given its present appearance under Napoleon I, who made it his private apartment. Later, under Louis-Philippe, it was lived in by the princesses Louise and Clémentine.

THE MUSIC ROOM

BARBIER, PARIS PARLIAMENTARY LAWYER, MAY 1750.
"[The King] also travels and stays two or three days at Trianon, in the park of Versailles, where small apartments have been built and decorated with the latest furniture. Trianon was once abandoned, and could only host few festivities, and serve a light meal after the Ladies' walk. But it now acts as a country home. These are built wherever possible in order to diversify the objects and trips, especially since the King has a tendency to be easily bored, and Madame de Pompadour's art is in her trying to amuse him."

THE ROUND DRAWING ROOM

ZEPHYR AND FLORA
BY ANTOINE COYPEL

LOUIS-PHILIPPE'S FAMILY DRAWING ROOM

After crossing the round drawing room, used as a chapel during Louis XV's reign, and then the Drawing room of Napoleon's Officers, one comes to Louis-Philippe's spacious family drawing room. This room was formed by connecting the Drawing room of Napoleon's High Officers and that of his Princes. Finally, the visitor may admire Napoleon's State Cabinet (formerly the Duchesse de Bourgogne's bedchamber). This room is called the Malachite Drawing room after the slabs of malachite given to the Emperor by Czar Alexander I. These ornaments stand on furniture executed in 1809 by Jacob Desmalter.

THE MALACHITE DRAWING ROOM

The reception suite is followed by the Cool Drawing room, the Gallery and the Garden Drawing room. The rooms in this suite (except for the Garden Drawing room) still display the paintings commissioned by Louis XIV from the painters Cotelle, Allegrain and Martin. All these works are dedicated to the portrayal of the buildings and, above all, the park of Versailles as they were during the reign of the Sun King. The Gallery has been named after Cotelle, whose works portray the gardens as the setting for mythological scenes. It links the main building of the château and the Trianon-in-the-Woods wing.

THE DRAWING ROOM OF THE SPRINGS

MADAME DE MAINTENON, LETTER TO MR. DE JUSSAC, AUGUST 8, 1689.
"The tuberose plants forced us to leave Trianon every night, much too early; but most of the men and women felt ill from too much perfume."

THE COTELLE GALLERY

The Cool Drawing room is followed by a series of small rooms which have, as far as possible, been refurnished as they were under the Empire; with the exception of the Study, entirely redecorated in 1813, the majority of the wainscotting dates from renovations made under Louis XV.

The most completely restored rooms are certainly the Emperor's bathroom and, particularly, his Bedchamber. Previously Louis XV's Council Chamber, this room once again contains its furniture by Baudouin, and its buff, lilac and silver silk moire wall hangings, originally designed for Empress Josephine at the Tuileries.

THE GAMES ROOM

FONTAINE (ARCHITECT FROM NAPOLEON TO LOUIS-PHILIPPE) - JOURNAL, MAY 31, 1808
"The Emperor, in a decision dated this May 26, has granted the sum of 212 thousand francs to renovate Trianon, supply the plans and unite the two gardens. Mr. Trepsat shall be in charge of the work as long as his health holds out, and if not, it will be Mr. Dufour, and both shall be under my supervision. We regard this declaration as a confirmation of the nomination of Dufour who is ready to go to work [...] He [Dufour] has made a few presentations and the Field Marshal [Duroc] while giving instructions for Trianon has asked that he be invited to tender projects for the renovation of the château of Versailles."

THE EMPEROR'S STUDY

EMPEROR'S BEDCHAMBER

Until 1703, the right front section contained the Theater, followed by Louis XIV's apartment, for which, in 1709, Boulle delivered the chest of drawers now in the Mercury Drawing room of the main château. Louis XV had a Games room, Dining room and Buffet room built here. These rooms continued to be used as such until 1845, when Louis-Philippe had them transformed for his daughter, the Queen of Belgium and her husband, Leopold I. Marie-Louise's former bed was brought here from the Tuileries, and two chests of drawers and a console table in the style of Boulle were added.

THE BELGIAN QUEEN'S BEDCHAMBER

QUEEN HORTENSE, DECEMBER 25, 1809. "He [the Emperor] went to Trianon and asked us [Hortense and Joséphine] to come and visit. I went along with my mother. This meeting was very touching. The Emperor wanted her to stay for dinner. As usual he was seated in front of her. Seemingly nothing had changed. The Queen of Naples and I were alone. The pages and the palace prefect were there as usual. The room was very quiet. My mother couldn't eat a thing and I could tell she was on the verge of fainting. The Emperor wiped his eyes two or three times without saying a word and we left immediately after dinner."

THE GRAND TRIANON'S GARDENS

For Louis XIV, the gardens at Trianon, like those of all his residences, had an extremely important role to play. Although they were badly treated towards the end of the 18th century, the original layout of the gardens still exists as designed by Le Bouteaux, Le Nôtre's nephew at the time of the Porcelain Trianon (1670-1687). When Trianon was rebuilt in 1687, all the gardens were rearranged by Le Nôtre until his death in 1700. Many groves remained unfinished and some of them were completed by Hardouin-Mansart. It was not until 1704 that some of the lead sculptures were first installed, most of them coming from groves rearranged in the park of Versailles.

The Upper Garden is adorned with two Languedoc marble pools in the center of which are groups of children by Girardon, formerly from the Banquet Hall taken down in 1706. These fountains are in the center of parterres whose Louis XIV floral embroidery was simplified under Louis XVI. The Lower Garden contains an octagonal reflection pool decorated with a group by Marsy: The *Child surrounded by Grapes*. It was here that, under Louis XIV, the orange trees and flowery shrubs, so greatly admired at the time, were set out.

At the south end of the Lower Garden, a balustrade overlooks the Horseshoe Fountain.

In the axis of the Peristyle, a wide avenue leads to the Mirror Fountain, adorned with groups of children. On its rims, two dragons by Hardy frame the edge of the upper level. Beyond this fountains stands the *Knifegrinder*, a marble statue in the classical style, set against trees which round off this view of the gardens.

To the north lies a small stretch of woodland with three main stars: the Small Star, the Great Star and the Queen's Star.

From the Mirror Fountain, an avenue leads to the grove of the Round Pool, situated in the axis of the Garden Drawing room.

Beyond the Round Pool, in the axis of the Trianon-in-the-Woods pavilion, stands the Water Buffet with its tiered basins designed by Jules Hardouin-Mansart. Carved out of white Carrara and red Languedoc marble, it is adorned with sculptures by Van Clève, Mazière, Le Lorrain, Poirier and Hardy. With Neptune and Amphitrite as its central theme, it is the only mythological group in the gardens of Trianon.

MARQUIS DE SOURCHES, JULY 23, 1685
On July 23, we celebrated at Versailles the wedding of the Duc de Bourbon with Mlle de Nantes; […] at 10 o'clock, the King landed at the foot of Trianon, and having come up through the garden, a wonderful supper was laid out on four different tables; it was served in the four rooms which looks onto the garden, all lit by a large number of crystal chandeliers. After supper the King sailed back on the canal […]"

THE GARDEN DRAWING ROOM

I am very well housed; I have four rooms and the cabinet from which I am writing. There is a view out to the springs, as the area is called. The springs are a small grove with so many trees that even the midday sun cannot penetrate. There are over fifty of these springs which form little rivulets about a foot wide, making them easy to walk over; they are edged by lawn and form little islands large enough to place a table and chairs, so that one can play in the shade. There are wide steps on either side, as everything here is on a bit of a slope […] the water also runs over the steps and forms a waterfall on either side. As you can tell, the spot is quite pleasant. On my side, the trees almost come into my windows; this is why the suite of rooms where the Princesse de Conti, Mr. le Dauphin, myself and Mme la Duchesse are housed, is called Trianon-in-the-woods."

**FACADE
OVERLOOKING
THE GRAND
TRIANON'S
UPPER GARDEN**

From the Water Buffet, we return through the Green Hall in the Chestnut garden to Trianon-in-the-Woods and, symmetrical to the Horseshoe in relation to the axis of the Gallery, we find the Hall of Classical Statues or Amphitheater. It still has its pool adorned with four nymphs and, at regular intervals along the semicircle, twenty-five busts copied from classical models.

After going through the end of Trianon-in-the-Woods, where we find a reflection pool with two half-moons and adorned with a faun attributed to Marsy, we come to the second part of the Trianon gardens.

Situated in the angle formed by the Gallery and the Trianon-in-the-Woods wing, the Garden of the Springs was a sort of Louis XIV prefiguration of the "English Garden". The Springs were unfortunately removed in 1776 and replaced by a simple parterre. Only the sculpture, Cupid on a dolphin by Marsy, placed here in 1704, remains.

Beyond this, and formerly separated from the rest of the gardens by a little wall, lies the former King's Garden. Although it was very badly damaged in the 18th century, it has retained its original appearance.

THE PETIT TRIANON

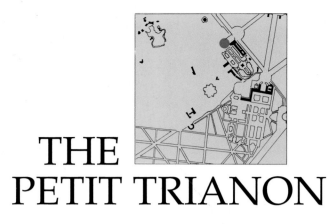

As early as 1761, Madame de Pompadour had suggested to Louis XV that a small château be erected in the French Garden. The project was to be carried out by Gabriel, and in 1768, the Petit Trianon was inaugurated.

A masterpiece of neoclassical architecture, it is undoubtedly Gabriel's most successful creation. The building, erected on a square ground plan, comprises a basement, a main floor, and an attic storey surmounted with a balustrade, concealing the Italian-style roof. Owing to variations in the ground level, the basement is only visible on the Main Courtyard side and on the side facing the Temple of Love. The facades are dotted with pilasters and powerful Corinthian columns.

Since the reign of Napoleon III, the first floor has been dedicated to the memory of Marie-Antoinette. Little by little, the furniture belonging either to the Queen herself or, failing that, to her furniture repository, has been returned to her little château. The paintings, however, are mainly those placed here during the reign of Louis XV. In the attic storey, in what was formerly the King's suite, the wall hangings in the bedchamber have been re-woven as they were in the 18th century, and the furniture, which once belonged to kings and princes, has been added.

The other rooms contain furnishings present in the Petit Trianon during the 19th century. These include commissions for Marie-Louise or the Duchesse d'Orléans, who succeeded each other in this estate but who have, to some extent, been forgotten.

THE PETIT TRIANON ON THE GARDEN SIDE

**THE RECEPTION
ROOM**

**BARONESS OF
OBERKIRCH,
MEMOIRS, ON THE
COURT OF LOUIS XVI**
"During my illness, a
great event occurred
at Versailles: the
Queen gave birth to
the Dauphin (Crown
Prince). He was
christened the day

following his birth by
the Cardinal, who is
the Prince of Rohan,
Grand Chaplain, and
Bishop of Strasbourg,
and was held over
the font in the name of
the Emperor and of
Madame de Piémont,
by Monsieur, the
King's eldest brother

and by the Countess
of Provence. It
became fashionable
to wear a golden
dolphin (the symbol
of France's crown
prince) adorned
with gemstones,
as one would
wear small gold
crosses."

**MARIE-
ANTOINETTE
WITH A ROSE**
**BY MADAME
VIGÉE-LEBRUN**

THE FRENCH PAVILION

In 1750, Gabriel built the French Pavilion. During his many visits to the new menagerie, Louis XV would often stop here and rest. The building has a cross-shaped ground plan with four cabinets surrounding a large circular drawing room. There is a charming simplicity about the exterior, the facades are varied by the shape of the cabinets jutting out, and topped by a balustrade adorned with sculptures (groups of children and flowered vases).

THE FRENCH PAVILION

MARIE-ANTOINETTE'S THEATER

Richard Mique finished building Marie-Antoinette's Theater next to the Petit Trianon in 1780. The interior decor recalls that of the Royal Opera in the château of Versailles. The ground plan is U-shaped; above the stage is a cartouche bearing Marie-Antoinette's monogram. The original ceiling, painted by Lagrenée, depicted Apollo in the company of the Muses and Graces. It has been replaced with a copy.

THE COMTE OF HÉZECQUES, RECOLLECTIONS OF A PAGE IN LOUIS XVI'S COURT
"In France, the Queen introduced an instrument, invented by Franklin and known as the harmonica or glasschord, whose sound is made by the impact of an infinite number of small rods striking glasses filled to various levels with water; the Queen could play it well, along with several other instruments.

[…] Marie-Antoinette had her own house, officers, pages, and livery, which was red and silver; but it was the King's guard who accompanied her. […] I never saw the Queen dance. At the end of the balls, those who had finished dancing allowed themselves to form an English promenade, and the Queen would join in; but I have heard that she danced very well. I saw for myself that she rode horseback with as much grace as daring. […] The Queen had lovely hair, of a very pleasant blonde color, which lent its name, some thirty years ago, to a shade very much in fashion."

MARIE-ANTOINETTE'S THEATER

THE BELVEDERE

In 1777, a neo-classical pavilion, the Belvedere, was erected by Mique on a mound commanding a view over the lake. Octagonal in shape, it is reached by four steps flanked by sphinxes. The sculptures on the frontons depict rustic pleasures, while the bas-reliefs symbolize the four seasons. The interior is paved with a marble mosaic. The arabesques on the stucco walls were painted by Le Riche, while the clear sky with fleeting clouds on the cupola is the work of Lagrenée.

THE TEMPLE OF LOVE

The Temple of Love was built by Mique on an islet of the river, opposite the windows of the Queen's Bedchamber. It consists of twelve white marble Corinthian columns, standing on a circular pedestal of seven steps, and surmounted by a cupola. In the middle stands a copy, executed by Bouchardon, of Cupid carving his bow out of Hercules' club. The original, sculpted in 1746, is now in the Louvre.

THE TEMPLE OF LOVE

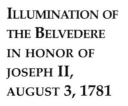

ILLUMINATION OF THE BELVEDERE IN HONOR OF JOSEPH II, AUGUST 3, 1781

MARIE-ANTOINETTE'S HAMLET

During the second half of the 18th century, Jean-Jacques Rousseau's theories on a "state of nature" were very much in fashion. These new ideas prompted Marie-Antoinette to create the Hamlet, a kind of fairyland village on the banks of the Grand Trianon lake. Built by Mique between 1783 and 1785, the village numbered twelve houses.

By walking along the left bank of the lake, the visitor will first discover the "Processing Dairy" and the Marlborough Tower with the Fishery underneath. The "Preparation Dairy" and the Barn, also used as a Ballroom, once stood nearby. Down the path is the guard's house and the dovecot. The bridge leads to the billiards rooms, linked to the Queen's house by a gallery. This is followed by the boudoir or Queen's smaller house and the Mill. The meticulously decorated interiors of the cottages in the Hamlet contrasted with the natural simplicity of the exteriors.

A real farm operated near the Hamlet: "Gardens were planted, fields were tilled, trees were pruned, and the fruit was picked. From her house the Queen could see the donkey bringing the grain to the mill […]", wrote Pierre de Nolhac. And Madame Campan says: "The pleasure of strolling through all the farmyard buildings of the Hamlet, of seeing the cows being milked, of fishing in the lake, enchanted the Queen."

THE MILL

The Malborough tower

The Queen's house

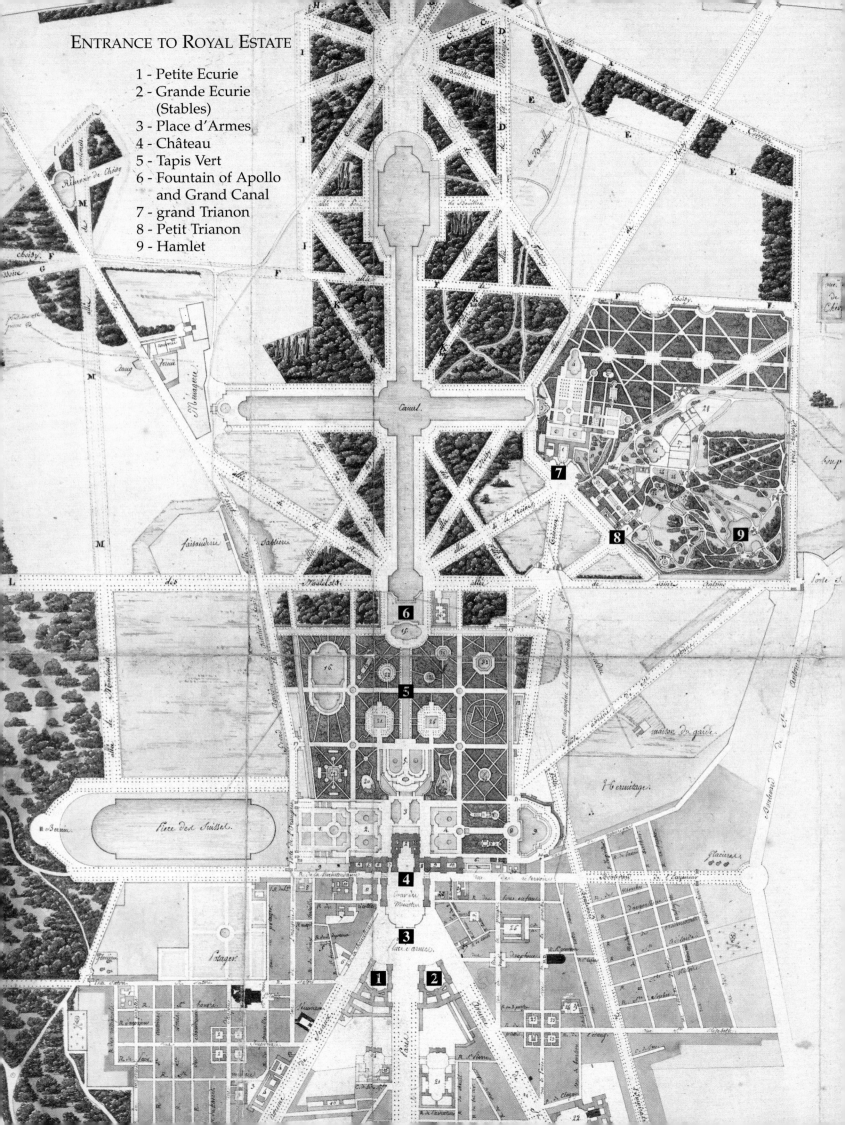

ENTRANCE TO ROYAL ESTATE

1 - Petite Ecurie
2 - Grande Ecurie
    (Stables)
3 - Place d'Armes
4 - Château
5 - Tapis Vert
6 - Fountain of Apollo
    and Grand Canal
7 - grand Trianon
8 - Petit Trianon
9 - Hamlet